A
MACABRE
MISCELLANY

A
MACABRE
MISCELLANY

One Thousand Grisly and Unusual Facts
from around the World

by

GEOFFREY ABBOTT

Yeoman Warder (retd), HM Tower of London
Member of The Sovereign's Bodyguard
of the Yeomen of the Guard Extraordinary

First published in 2004 by
Virgin Books Ltd
Thames Wharf Studios
Rainville Road
London
W6 9HA

A catalogue record for this book is available from
the British Library.

ISBN 07535 08494

Typeset by Phoenix Photosetting, Chatham, Kent
Printed and bound in Great Britain by Bookmarque

CONTENTS

THIS BOOK IS DEDICATED TO ALL THOSE WHO ENJOY
KNOWING SOME FACTS ABOUT MANY SUBJECTS
RATHER THAN THOSE WHO PREFER TO KNOW A GREAT DEAL
ABOUT A FEW.

INTRODUCTION

It was not until I was privileged to become a Yeoman Warder ('Beefeater') of the Tower of London that I realised how over-whelmingly fascinated members of the general public are by matters macabre. Admittedly, some of the two-and-a-half million or so visitors to the Tower each year had come to study the Tudor architecture, to marvel at the Crown Jewels, to pose for photo-graphs with me or my colleagues as mementos of their holiday, even to savour the experience of actually being in a royal palace, but judging by the questions posed by the vast majority, the shudder-making topics of torture and execution were uppermost in their minds: where was the torture chamber?, can we see the axe, the block? where was Anne Boleyn executed? what did they do with her head? and so on.

Their seemingly inexhaustible thirst for lurid information could only be satisfied by researching the bizarre episodes in the Tower's history, researches which inevitably included the study of torture and execution in general. Over the years this provided me with material for numerous books and, aware that the public's ghoulish curiosity was not limited solely to those subjects but also to occurrences of any description – as long as they included elements of weird behaviour – I spread my net wider, amassing a large collection of grotesque events, one thousand of which I now present for your diversion and delectation. So, connoisseurs of off-beat happenings – read on and enjoy!

BONES, BRAINS AND BODY PARTS

Adolf Hitler's jawbone was reportedly extracted from his burned corpse in Berlin in 1945 and is now held in the Russian Federation Archives in Moscow.

The teaching of anatomy in colonial America was hindered by the shortage of live specimens. Judge Samuel Sewell wrote in his diary for 22 September 1676, 'Spent the day from nine in the morning with Mr Brackenbury, dissecting the middle-most part of the Indian executed the day before. He took the heart in his hand and affirmed it to be the stomach!'

One of Napoleon's teeth was bought at auction by an American in 1995 for £3910.

In the 1780s the corpses of hanged Dutch criminals were left suspended from the gallows for many months as deterrents, until eventually their disintegrating flesh and body parts dropped into deep holes dug beneath the scaffold for that purpose.

Late in the nineteenth century H.H. Holmes, a Canadian serial killer, buried some of his victims in a cellar but ingeniously disposed of them later: having dug up the corpses, he persuaded a medical friend to connect the bones in their correct order, then sold the skeletons to a surgical school.

The jawbone of Richard II was stolen from its tomb in Westminster Abbey in the early 1800s by a schoolboy attending the nearby Westminster School. He took it home and his father, far from chastising his sacrilegious son, mounted it in a glass case and proudly labelled it 'Jawbone of Richard II'. In 1916 it passed into the possession of a clergyman, who returned it to the authorities.

Before severed heads were displayed in public on London Bridge, they were preserved by being parboiled in salt water and cumin seed to deter the sea birds from eating the flesh.

William Corder, the 'Red Barn murderer', was skinned after being hanged on 11 August 1828. The pieces of skin were then sold as souvenirs.

Although St Thomas More's body is interred in the Chapel Royal of St Peter ad Vincula in the Tower of London, his head is entombed in St Dunstan's Church, Canterbury.

Lady Raleigh kept the severed head of her husband, Sir Walter Raleigh, preserved in a case for the remaining 29 years of her life; it then passed to their son Carew and is believed to have been buried with him at West Horsley, Surrey.

Putrefaction houses were stone buildings in cemeteries in which corpses were kept until they had putrefied, in order to defeat bodysnatchers, whose object was to dig them up and sell them to surgical schools.

In the Great Depression of the 1930s, Americans living in the South made a meagre living by digging up Indian remains and selling the skulls to tourists as souvenirs.

Newspaper editors in the late 1960s devoted many column inches to reports that graves had been violated in cemeteries in Tottenham Park, London, and Clophill, Bedfordshire, and that some of their gruesome contents had allegedly been used by Satanists celebrating the Black Mass – for which human nails, teeth, hair and fragments of flesh are necessary constituents.

On 14 September 1602, when George Praun was executed in Nuremberg, it was reported by the executioner that 'when placed on a stone his head turned several times as if it wanted to look about it, moved its tongue and opened its mouth as if wanting to speak, for a good half quarter of an hour'.

When Oliver Cromwell died in 1658, his corpse was embalmed so inefficiently that, as his doctor later reported, 'the filth broke through, and it was prudent to bury him immediately, which was done in as private a manner as possible.'

In ancient Egypt the most expensive method of embalming involved making an incision in the abdomen wall. The viscera (organs) were removed and placed in clay or alabaster vases, and the brain was extracted with a hook inserted through the nostrils. Next, all cavities were filled with spices and the body was soaked for seventy days in a salt solution; it was then coated with gum, wrapped in a cloth, placed in a wooden coffin and deposited in a burial chamber. The vases containing the viscera were placed nearby.

For refusing to accept Henry VIII as head of the Church in England, Fr John Houghton, Prior of the London Charterhouse, was hanged, drawn and quartered in 1535 and one of his arms was nailed over the Charterhouse gate as a warning to all. Two of the young monks retrieved it, intending to send it abroad as a holy relic, only to be caught – and they themselves executed in a similar gory fashion.

After Napoleon's death his body was interred on St Helena, his heart was placed in a silver vase of spirits and buried separately; later, both corpse and heart were removed and buried in Paris with full honours.

After decapitation, the head of Oliver Plunket, RC Primate of Ireland, became a holy relic in Siena Convent, Drogheda, Ireland.

Even as recently as the nineteenth century in England, members of the public were allowed to watch the dissection of human bodies.

Satirist Jonathan Swift (1667–1745), Dean of St Paul's, Dublin, spent his life attacking the Establishment and the sins of society. Doubts arose as to his sanity and, when he died, his skull was opened up. It was reported that 'the sinus of the cranium was loaded with water.'

During the Diocletian persecution, Juanarius, Bishop of Benevento, was thrust into a white-hot furnace but sustained no injuries; he was then thrown into a cage full of wild beasts but the animals refrained from attacking him, so he was decapitated by his foes. Martyred, he became the patron saint of Naples, his head being preserved in a church in that city, together with two phials of his blood. When the three holy relics are brought close together, it is said that the congealed blood liquefies and bubbles.

When Canadian Willie Wells' head was crushed beneath a heavy weight, the authorities sought to prove the guilt of the suspects, the Hyams twins, at their murder trial in 1895 by cleaning the skull, re-assembling it, using copper wire, then producing it in court.

After many vicissitudes Oliver Cromwell's head was finally buried in the grounds of a Cambridge college in 1960.

The French equivalent to Tyburn was Montfaucon, sited not far from Paris. Not only hangings took place there, but the body parts of men who had been decapitated, torn to pieces by horses or boiled to death, or had committed suicide, were hung up in sacks of sackcloth or leather and left to rot or be devoured by flocks of birds.

Before his death in 1928 the renowned author Thomas Hardy stated that he wished to be buried in Stinsford Churchyard, near Dorchester. Part of his wish was carried out, in that his heart was interred there, in a carved casket, but his fame was such that his body now rests in Poets' Corner, Westminster Abbey.

A list of allegedly holy relics once revered in Westminster Abbey includes some of St Stephen's bones; the greater part of one of the nails of Our Saviour's Cross; parts of the sponge, lance and scourge with which he was tortured; many pieces of the vestments of the Virgin Mary, and some of her milk and hair; hairs of St Peter's beard, and one of St Paul's fingers.

Dom Bede Camm in his book *Forgotten Shrines* described the skull of Ven. Charles Baker S.J., which is now a holy relic, as containing the skeleton of a mouse which apparently had made a nest there; when the skull was placed in a box, the mouse could not escape.

Henry Grey, Duke of Suffolk, was decapitated on the orders of Queen Mary for being involved in uprisings in support of his daughter, Lady Jane Grey. His head was buried in the chapel of the family home near the Tower of London. When the house was eventually demolished, the head was found to be remarkably preserved because it had fallen, when severed by the axe, into a basket containing oak sawdust. It was later put in a glass case and kept in St Botolph's Church, Aldgate, where, for a small fee, the vicar would produce it to be viewed. An offer by an American collector to buy it for £500 was rejected, and some time after World War II it was reverently buried beneath the paving stones in front of the church.

Authors guilty of publishing seditious libel ran appalling risks during the reign of Elizabeth I. One George Stubbs ran foul of the law and was sentenced to have his writing hand chopped off at the wrist with a meat cleaver. As the amputation took place George, patriotic almost beyond belief, took off his hat with his left hand and shouted 'God save the Queen!'

Mutilation for following the 'wrong' religion was widespread in the American colonies. The Massachusetts Colonial Records for 1657 reveal that 'A Quaker, if male, for the first offense shall have one of his eares cutt off; for the second offense have his other ear cutt off; a woman shalbe severely whipt; for the third offense they, he or she, shall have their tongues bored through with a hot iron.'

The poet John Milton died in 1674 and sixteen years later a grave believed to be his was opened. The grave robbers pulled locks of hair from the skull and, using a stick, knocked some of the teeth out, to keep as souvenirs.

The last ceremonial interment of a heart in England was that of Paul Whitehead, secretary to the monks of Medmenham, Buckinghamshire; the organ was buried in the mausoleum at High Wycombe.

In 1632 one William Prynne paid the penalty for criticising the royal family by having his ears amputated. One hopes he didn't need to wear glasses!

'Resurrection Men' were not priests, but grave robbers.

In eighteenth-century America, dissection of the human body, even for instructional purposes, filled the general public with horror. This culminated in April 1788 in New York, when Dr Richard Bayle, working on a specimen in a hospital laboratory, noticed a small boy looking through the window and jocularly he waved one of the corpse's arms at him. Attracted by the lad's screams, a mob gathered, attacked the building, destroyed the anatomical remains and surrounded the jail in which the medical staff had taken refuge. The local militia were called out and, in the battle that ensued, seven rioters were killed and many more wounded. This fracas resulted in the New York State Legislature authorising the dissection of any criminals who had been executed for arson, murder or burglary.

St Agattin was killed by having her breasts cut off, so she is associated with diseases in that part of the female anatomy and is also the patron saint of nursing women. Similarly St Apollonia had her teeth forcibly removed, so prayers are directed to her by those suffering from toothache. Paintings portray her holding either a tooth or, perhaps even more appropriately, a pair of pincers.

Too long a rope had disastrous results when American Tom Ketchum was hanged in April 1901, for his head was torn off, fell and rolled on across the ground. The torso stayed upright for one horrific moment, then swayed and collapsed, blood gushing from the ruptured neck.

The heart of Richard I was buried in Rouen Cathedral, France, his intestines in Chaluz and his corpse at Fontevrault.

The heart of the martyr Ven. Edward Morgan was saved from the pyre near the scaffold and is said to be preserved in a

Teignmouth, Devon, place of worship. The holy relic, believed to be 2½ins in length, nearly 2ins in breadth at its widest and 1½ins thick, is enclosed in a heart-shaped cardboard box just large enough to contain it.

A descendant of St Thomas More, who was beheaded on the orders of Henry VIII, became a nun and later Prioress of the English Convent, Bruges, to which she bequeathed a holy relic, a vertebra of the saint's neck.

Being hanged, drawn and quartered involved the victim first being hanged, then cut down while still alive; following which he was castrated (symbolically, to ensure that he could not have children as treasonable as himself) and 'drawn', his stomach being slit open and his organs torn out; his heart was then displayed to the crowd. He was then decapitated and his body cut into quarters, the parts being publicly exhibited as deterrents.

The container into which a guillotine victim's head fell was known by those at the ringside as the 'Family Picnic Basket'.

On 3 September 1588 George Solen of Nuremberg was hanged for theft, but after eight days someone cut down half the body, doubtless for any money in the breeches pockets, and left the upper half hanging. It was reported that what was left of the corpse was thrown into the gallows pit the next day 'because it looked too horrible'.

The severed hand of Margaret Clitheroe, pressed to death at York in 1586, is preserved as a revered relic in the Old Bar Convent there. It lacks the joint of one finger, which was severed and presented to the donor, Mr Charles Weld.

John Fisher, Bishop of Rochester, was executed for denying

Henry VIII's claim to be supreme head of the Church of England but, before being parboiled and piked on London Bridge, his head was first shown to the woman whose place on the throne he had long disputed, Queen Anne Boleyn. The historian Holinshed reported that 'the pope had created him a Cardinal and sent his Cardinal's hat as far as Calis; but his hed was off before his hat was on – so they met not!'

An English naval captain's ear, severed by Spaniards who boarded his ship at sea, was the direct cause of the War of Jenkins' Ear in 1731.

The two bones which accompany the skull on the 'Jolly Roger' flag are thigh-bones.

The body of the martyr St John Southworth was sewn back together after having been hanged, drawn and quartered.

Simon de Montfort's corpse was mutilated after his death in battle at Evesham in 1235 by being beheaded and castrated, 'his privy members fastened upon either side of his nose and presented to the wife of the victor, Sir Roger Mortimer'.

Edward Gein dug up at least fifteen corpses in Wisconsin in 1957, skinning some of them and keeping the body parts and organs in a refrigerator. Progressing to murder, he killed two women; when caught, he was diagnosed as criminally insane and placed in an appropriate institution. Such was the evil reputation of the farm on which he had lived that it was burned down by neighbours.

In medieval Germany traitors were quartered and their remains spiked on the city's gates. At one time, women sentenced to death for child murder were decapitated and their heads nailed above the gallows.

9

A useful recipe appeared in the *Stamford Mercury* newspaper in October 1858, when it was reported that a woman had implored the local vicar 'for ever so small a fragment of human skull' so that she could grate it into a powder and add it to the medicine she was giving her daughter, who suffered from fits.

Mummification, as practised by the Peruvians, consisted of first freezing the corpses in snow, then coating them with a resinous substance.

In the eighteenth century, Temple Bar, an archway straddling Fleet Street, London, was occasionally adorned with the severed heads of traitors. The longest to be displayed there was that of Christopher Layer, whose shrivelled and blackened skull peered down at passers-by for more than thirty years. To those desirous of a closer view of the grim remains, entrepreneurs would hire out telescopes at a halfpenny a look.

In the same way as American Indians would scalp their defeated enemies in early centuries, so victorious Germans and Scandinavians would deprive their fallen enemies of their skulls as trophies.

Sir John Barkstead, MP for Colchester, was appointed by Oliver Cromwell as Lieutenant of the Tower of London, where he fleeced the Royalist prisoners for extra privileges and buried the proceeds in butter firkins within the grounds. When Charles II regained the throne in 1660, Barkstead fled but was recaptured and decapitated, and his head was impaled on a pole over Traitors' Gate. But no one ever found the gold!

In the early eighteenth century bodysnatchers would exhume corpses and sell them to surgical schools. The price of an adult cadaver was usually about four guineas (£4.20), while a child's was sold by length: 6s. (30p) for the first 12 inches, then 9d. (4p) an inch after that.

Execution by the axe was the judicial method in Hanover, Germany, in the last century, as butcher Fritz Haarmann found to his cost following his grisly series of crimes. Inviting young men to his apartment, he would ply them with drink until they were unconscious, bite their throats so that they bled to death, then dismember their bodies and sell the flesh over the counter as pork. The more succulent parts of their cadavers would become the ingredients of his special recipe for black pudding. Haarmann was decapitated in Hanover Prison on 19 December 1924; the reactions of his nauseated former customers were not recorded, but can be imagined.

One of the traditional Seven Wonders of the World was the Mausoleum built by Artemisia, Queen of Carla (352–350 BC) for her husband Mausolus. However, his body was not buried therein: instead it was burned and the ashes stirred into a glass of wine, which the Queen then drank to bring her husband closer to her than ever before.

African explorer David Livingstone died on 30 April 1873, alone except for his native bearers and servants. So devoted were they that they took it in turns to carry his body through deserts and over swamps until they reached the coast, where the remains were taken by ship to England – a year having passed before he was finally buried.

During the 1745 Jacobite Uprising, Captain James Dawson was one of the Scottish supporters condemned to be hanged, drawn and quartered. The execution took place on Kennington Common, London, on the day originally planned for his marriage. His fiancée could not be dissuaded from attending and, after watching the awful spectacle, seated herself in her coach – and died.

After Charles Guiteau, assassin of the American president James Garfield, had been hanged, his brain was extracted, clinically examined, and photographed in detail.

The heart of Robert Bruce, King of Scotland, was buried in Melrose Abbey.

The *London Magazine* of September 1735 reported that a seaman sentenced to death for wife-murder had poisoned himself in his cell. The locals, enraged at thus being deprived of watching him being hanged, 'proceeded to dig up his corpse where it had been buried at the cross-roads, dragged his viscera about the highway, picked his eyes out and broke almost all his bones.'

On 30 January 1661, twelve years to the day after Charles I had been beheaded, his son Charles II had the satisfaction of ordering that the cadavers of three of the leading figures responsible for his father's 'murder', Cromwell, Ireton and Bradshaw, be exhumed from their splendid tombs in Westminster Abbey, taken to Tyburn and hanged. The 'twice dead' bodies were then decapitated, the torsos buried beneath the gallows, and the heads stuck on spikes atop Westminster Hall.

After executions at Tyburn in the eighteenth century, violent fights frequently broke out between victims' relatives, who wanted to give the deceased a decent burial, and those sent to collect the corpses for delivery to surgeons to use as dissection specimens for their students.

Diamonds might be a girl's best friend, but the really valuable ones brought pain, even death, to those who possessed them. In the 1700s the Koh-i-Nur was owned by the Afghan leader Sjah Rokh, but when overthrown by Aga Mohammed he refused to disclose its whereabouts, despite being racked, torn with red-hot pincers and blinded with a lancet. Further persuasion was then applied, Aga had his captive's head shaved and encircled with a ring of paste, and hot oil was poured into the receptacle thus formed. Sjah was rescued by the founder of the Afghan dynasty, Ahmed Shah, who was given the gem; it later passed to a descendant, Zaman, who in turn forfeited his eyesight for possession of the Koh-i-Nur to his brother Shah Shuja. After a long history of torture and suffering, the precious stone was brought to England and now has an honoured place in the crown worn by the late Queen Mother; tradition has it that it will never bring misfortune again – as long as it is worn only by a woman.

Following his gruesome execution in the sixteenth century, the severed head of the Roman Catholic martyr Fr John Cornelius was used as a football by the bigoted mob at Dorchester before it was displayed above the city gates.

When the Scottish leader William Wallace was betrayed to Edward I in 1305, he was hanged, drawn and quartered and his head was impaled on a pike on London Bridge. At a cost of 61s. 10d. his quarters were taken north, where his right arm was displayed on a gibbet in Newcastle on Tyne, his left arm in Berwick, his right leg in Perth and his left leg in Aberdeen – all with the adjoining part of his torso still attached.

Henry I died 'of a surfeit of lampreys' in Normandy in 1135. His bowels, brain and eyes were buried in Rouen, while the rest of his body was powdered with salt and wrapped in bulls' hides 'because of the stink which poisoned those who stood near the corpse'. So toxic was the odour that the surgeon who was required to decapitate the corpse and remove the brain died.

On 1 June 1630 Guglielmo Piazza, Commissioner for Health in Milan, walked down a street writing from an ink-horn at his waist and was seen by local women to wipe his inky fingers on a nearby wall. They accused him of spreading the plague which was then raging in Italy and he was arrested and tortured so severely that he confessed and incriminated two others. The three were torn with red-hot pincers and had their right hands severed, then all were burned. Their ashes were thrown into the river and the house that Piazza had touched was demolished, a 'column of infamy' being erected on its site to commemorate the men who were supposed to have spread the dreaded plague.

During the persecution of English Roman Catholic martyrs in the early 1640s, the Spanish Ambassador, Count Egmont, took it upon himself to collect as many holy relics as possible from the places of their executions. He amassed a considerable number, among them the heart of secular priest William Ward, a thumb, a piece of burned lung and a part of a kidney of Fr Bartholomew Roe, the diaphragm, liver and two fingers of Ven. Thomas Bolliquer, a toe and a piece of Ven. Paul of St Magdalen's windpipe and the right-hand quarter of Ven. Francis Bell.

In the 1800s one of Napoleon's teeth was exhibited in Madame Tussaud's Museum in London.

When multiple murderer Edward Pritchard was hanged on 28 July 1865 he was wearing a fashionable pair of elastic-sided boots. During excavations in the prison grounds nearly fifty years later, his skeleton was uncovered. Most of his clothing had rotted away, but his boots remained in pristine condition. They were promptly stolen.

Peter Reyn-Bardt neglected to study local history before murdering his wife in 1960 and burying her in the garden of his house on the outskirts of Manchester. He later moved away, but, in 1983, a woman's skull was discovered in the area and, on being shown the remains, Reyn-Bart admitted his guilt and was sentenced to prison for life. It was not until some time later that further examination of the skull revealed it to be that of a woman who had died somewhat earlier than Mrs Reyn-Bardt – in AD 410.

In 1884 the yacht *Mignonette* sank off the Cape of Good Hope and three men, Dudley, Stephens and Brooks, together with seventeen-year-old Richard Parker, took to the only lifeboat. Twenty days later, when the men were starving, it was decided that the boy, by then weak from drinking seawater and from lack of food, would have to be sacrificed and, after a prayer, Stephens cut Parker's throat. They fed on his flesh until rescued three days later by a passing ship. Dudley and Stephens were subsequently found guilty of murder and cannibalism – Brooks, who had not agreed to the murder but had eaten some of the flesh, was not charged – but the death sentences were later commuted to six months' imprisonment.

Torture instruments suffered by blasphemers and heretics in the Middle Ages included the Iron Mouth Opener, which prevented the victim from closing his mouth, while the Tongue Tearer, a long pair of tongs, was used to tear the tongue out by the roots.

When thousands of corpses were being dug up all over the country by bodysnatchers and sold as dissection specimens, a Dundee man devised an ingenious method of deterring the villains – permanently – from stealing the body of his dead child, by installing 'a small box inclosing some deathful apparatus, communicating by means of wires with the four corners, to be fastened on top of the coffin'. Immediately before it was lowered into the earth, a large quantity of gunpowder was poured into the box, and the hidden mechanism put into a state of readiness, so that if anyone attempted to raise the coffin, he would be blown up. It was reported that the sexton seemed to dread an immediate explosion, for he started back in alarm after throwing in the first shovelful of earth.

Assassin Leon Czolgosz murdered the American president William McKinley in September 1901 while attending a reception; his bandaged right hand concealed a gun which he fired when the President reached out to shake hands with him. Czolgosz died in the electric chair, sulphuric acid being poured over the corpse to destroy all traces of him.

In the early nineteenth century a Professor Aldini demonstrated his 'galvanic process' by passing an electric current through the corpse of the murderer George Foster. Those present watched in horror as the cadaver's lips started moving and its limbs twitching; when one eye opened, an official of the Barber Surgeon Company, Mr Pass, went home and died from a heart attack.

In 1935, a shark which had been caught and presented to a Sydney aquarium suddenly regurgitated an arm. Tattoos on the limb, portraying two boxers sparring, afforded identification of the victim, and the rope entwining it suggested murder, but the man suspected of the crime was shot under suspicious circumstances – and the shark itself died shortly afterwards.

Death sentences were handed out to any slave committing murder in America. In 1712, one such read: 'he be carryed to the place of execution and there to be burned with a slow fire, that he may continue in torment for eight or ten hours & continued burning in the said fire until he be dead and consumed to ashes.'

During the Chinese Uprising of 1927–28, many victims suffered death by a thousand cuts. In this the executioner used a number of sharp knives to skilfully sever portions of flesh and limbs, taking great care not to end his victim's life prematurely; removal of breasts, hips, thighs, nose and ears would be followed by severing the hands, feet and legs. So methodical was the execution that four or five minutes would elapse before the executioner ended the appalling torture by thrusting his knife through the victim's heart.

Before the invention of false teeth, those who could afford it paid large sums of money to have their sugar-rotted ivory castles replaced by real molars. These were obtained from body-snatchers, others from 'sutlers', men who accompanied the army fighting in the various campaigns of the Napoleonic Wars. Some sutlers would not only steal money and valuables from the bodies strewn around after a battle but also gouge out their teeth for subsequent disposal. The fact that a victim might be only wounded was no deterrent; the ghouls would quickly silence any protests.

The rebellious son of King Charles the Bald of France was sentenced by the Parliament of Senlis in AD 873 to be deprived of his sight. This was usually done by passing a red-hot iron before the eyes 'until they were cooked', plunging a steel point into the pupils or plucking each eye from its socket.

In the 1750s relatives of those who had just died would hold a 'wake' – keep vigil over the corpse for a few days before burial – but occasionally they would opt out of it and hand the responsibility over to the nurses who had attended to the dear departed. As there was much demand for cadavers at that time for use as specimens by surgical schools, two women, Helen Torrence and Jean Waldie, saw the opportunity to solve their

17

cash flow problems and went into business: volunteering to 'wake' for customers, they would extract the corpse, close the coffin up again, sell the body to the surgeons and of course charge the relatives for their services. Both entrepreneurial ladies were later caught and hanged.

Among the French Huguenots who were burned alive on 21 January 1535 in the presence of the King was a man named Antoine Poile who had his tongue first pierced, then pulled out of his mouth and attached to his cheek with an iron pin.

Those who exhumed bodies from cemeteries did so in order to sell them to surgeons for cash, but an extraordinary case arose in November 1828 when a surgeon was arrested for breaking into a vault in Hendon and not only stealing his own mother's corpse but beheading it! He explained in court that his family suffered from a hereditary disease and, by dissecting his mother's head, he thought he might have been able to establish its nature and cause. Although his purpose was laudable, his deed was a crime, and he was suitably punished.

The notorious highwayman Dick Turpin was hanged in York in 1739, then buried in an unusually deep grave to thwart body-snatchers, but they were determined to obtain the corpse and sell it to a surgical school, so they dug it up. However, the empty hole was noticed, the alarm raised and the corpse found dumped in a nearby surgeon's garden. This time the authorities were determined that Turpin's corpse should go down and stay down, so it was replaced in the coffin, which was then filled with unslaked lime, buried even deeper than before and guarded by relays of watchers, until time and lime had done their work.

'Mortsafes', as the name implies, were railed cages erected round graves to prevent grave robbers from digging up fresh corpses in order to sell them to surgeons for instructional purposes. The cages were removed and reused after putrefaction was assumed to have taken place.

The cost of an exhumation is usually borne by local authorities. One undertaker's bill submitted in 1933 read: Rope, 6s.; Line, 12s. 6d.; Undertaker's expenses, £6.6s.; Men's services, each, £1; Use of room, £2; Use of horse £2; and four bottles of whisky, £2.10s. – for, as the undertaker said at the time, he wouldn't do the same or a similar job for £50!

In September 2003 the French Government admitted that when the temperature rose to a record 40°C (104°F) between 1 and 15 August, the number of deaths in the country rose to 11,435, far in excess of the average number for that month in previous years. Mainly those aged over sixty died from the heat, and in many cases their bodies were not discovered until relatives returned from their traditional August holiday.

When George Frederick Cooke, a well-known eighteenth-century actor, died, his doctor, John Francis, decapitated his corpse and kept the head for research purposes. When the body was buried in St Paul's churchyard in New York, the absence of the head was discovered. Dr Francis denied all knowledge of its whereabouts, but after his death it eventually passed into the possession of Dr Ross Patterson of Jefferson Medical College, Philadelphia. A century later, the then owner arranged for it to be returned to the coffin, and research later revealed its whereabouts during the intervening years: the only place an actor's head could be – as a skull used on stage by the renowned actor Edwin Booth in countless performances of *Hamlet*. Alas, poor Yorick!

In the late thirteenth century, between fifteen and twenty thousand Jews were expelled from England. When a ship carrying hundreds of them reached the mouth of the Thames, the captain dropped anchor and, as the tide ebbed, persuaded the passengers to take a walk on the sands. When they did so, he sailed with the tide, and the rising waters drowned those left marooned. At the place where they perished, it is said that there is a never-ending bubbling of the waters. In the early years of the twentieth century, some East End Jews, on a certain date each year, would charter a boat and row out to the spot, there to wail and pray while they watched for the bubbles to rise over the watery graves of their ancestors.

In old Siam, when a new city was being built, it was the custom for certain officers to lie in wait and seize the first four or five passers-by, then have them buried alive under the gate-posts, where they became guardian angels of the entrance.

Although bodysnatchers are rightly condemned and abhorred, on at least one occasion their activities were more than welcomed: on 15 April 1824, by one John Macintire, who later wrote: 'I had been some time ill of a low and lingering fever. One day I was seized with strange and indescribable quiverings. I tried to move but could not; I heard the sound of weeping at my pillow and the voice of the nurse saying, "He is dead." I exerted my utmost power to stir myself but could not move even an eyelid. My father drew his hand over my face and closed my eyelids. I heard my friends speak in low accents, and felt myself placed in the coffin and borne away.' He then felt it lowered into the grave and the clatter of soil falling on it, then silence. This is death, he thought, and soon the worms will be crawling about my flesh. Later he heard a low sound, the coffin moved and he was dragged out; he heard rough men talking and was carried some distance. He felt himself placed on a table and, unable to move, heard the sounds of nurses bustling about, of doctors and students assembling. He continued: 'When all was ready, the Demonstrator took his knife and pierced my breast; I felt a dreadful cracking throughout my whole frame; a convulsive shudder of my body instantly followed, and a shriek of horror rose from all present. My terrible trance was ended; the utmost exertions were made to restore me, and in the course of an hour I was in full possession of all my faculties.' Of such accounts are nightmares made!

As recently as 1872 there was a scare in Calcutta when the Hooghly Bridge was being built, because of a rapidly spreading rumour that Mother Ganges, indignant at being thus crossed, had at last consented to submit to the insult – on condition that each piece of the structure would be founded on a layer of children's heads.

Trepanning (surgery on the skull) is the earliest operation of which any evidence has been discovered in ancient skeletons. In order (it was believed) to release demons, a hole would be made in the skull, using a flint, until the thin grey membrane appeared; then great care had to be taken for, if that was damaged, the demon would be enraged and the patient would die. However, once that had been gently penetrated, the demon would escape unseen and the patient would survive.

The famous diarist Samuel Pepys suffered the debilitating and painful ailment of a stone in the urinary tract. When it was surgically removed, he had it specially mounted in an elegant box. On 1 May each year he would give a party and invite others of his friends who had had the same operation; together they would discuss their separate ordeals and compare notes – and stones!

Holy relics, not all of them authentic, were much sought after in the Middle Ages. Henry VII's prize possession was the left leg of Saint George.

Even as recently as the nineteenth century the belief existed that a person's corpse should be complete when facing his or her

Maker, and so milk teeth or any others extracted during their lifetime were retained and, eventually, placed in the dead person's hand in the coffin. There was, seemingly, no equivalent ruling regarding amputated limbs!

The caravan route across the Gobi Desert was constantly traversed in the sixteenth century by rich merchants transporting their goods to Peking and beyond. They were constantly ambushed and robbed by bandits, until some of the latter were captured and buried alive, with only their heads protruding above the sand, thereby marking both the route for lawful travellers and the fate of those attempting to rob them.

Nineteenth-century coffin makers came up with the idea of making heavy cast-iron coffins to prevent bodysnatchers from digging them up or breaking into them and stealing the corpses, but at the horrific prospect of cemeteries full of non-biodegradable caskets, the authorities quickly rejected the proposal.

The great Cardinal Richelieu of France died in 1642, but in 1793 the revolutionists dug up the body; the head was cut off and later bought by a M. Armaz. In 1866 the relic was handed in to the Sorbonne where, with appropriate rites, it was deposited. But then M. Armaz's claim was disputed by someone else, who claimed that he had the authentic head. Bizarrely enough, M. Armaz had the face, while the other person had the rest of the head!

In 1601, during Elizabeth I's reign, a German traveller, Paul Hentzner, visited London and observed later that he had seen 'three hundred gory heads stuck up on London Bridge, and a great number spiked in various places about the Tower'.

A suicide bomber killed twenty Israelis in a Haifa restaurant in October 2003. A severed head with long black hair, found afterwards in the debris, was identified as that of the woman who had detonated the bomb she carried.

Two hours after French criminal Menesclau had been guillotined in 1907, Doctor Amirault connected a live dog to the severed head and proceeded to pump some of the canine's blood into it. Watchers were fascinated as Menesclau's ashen complexion slowly regained its normal colour, the lips trembled and the eyelids flickered, although after a few seconds all apparent signs of life disappeared, leaving the medical scientists to draw whatever conclusions they could.

When, in 1757, the Florentine physician Cocchi was entrusted with the removal of the remains of the astronomer Galileo to the Church of Santa Croce in Florence, he stole the fifth lumbar vertebra; the bone, which is about the size of a boy's fist, is now held in the Padua museum.

After the death in December 1882 of Léon Michel Gambetta, leading politician and once dictator of France, reportedly from a gunshot wound to the hand, a post mortem was carried out in the presence of some learned professors. Four of them took souvenirs home: Professor Cornil got the viscera, M. Lannelongue the cadaver's wounded right arm, M. Duval, President of the Société d'Anthropologie, appropriated the brain and M. Bertin carried off the heart.

When young, the Count de Frontenac married the girl of his dreams, but the union turned sour. Later he was appointed French Governor of Canada. Despite his wife not accompanying him, he retained the old affection he had always felt for her and when, in 1698, he was about to die, he requested that his heart be removed and proffered to her as a lasting tribute. After his death it was enclosed in a lead box and shipped back to France, but alas, the lady spurned the gift, saying that she did not want a dead heart which, when beating, had not belonged to her. So the pitiful relic was returned to Canada and buried with the Count's body in the chapel of Recollets, Quebec.

After the victims of the French Revolution had been guillotined, many of the corpses were taken to the town of Meudon, where experts at the craft skinned them. The skins were then flayed, the end-product being a superb soft leather, ideal for belts and even breeches. Men's skins were said to be superior in toughness and quality to chamois leather, but those of women were too soft to be of much use.

Unsuspected by the hundreds of thousands of tourists who had walked across his last resting place, a skeleton was discovered fifteen feet down during excavations in the Inner Ward of the Tower of London in 1976. Seen by the author, the skeleton lay in a hole too short for him, his knees bent as if he had been lowered gently into his 'grave'. That his death must have been a violent one was evidenced by the gaping hole in his skull; the remains were taken away and dated to about AD 70.

The American cemetery containing the remains of twenty thousand slaves was closed in 1794, but, when offices were being built in Manhattan, the remains of a further 419 slaves were discovered. In 2003 these were reverently re-interred near the site of the New York market where, centuries ago, having disembarked from the slave-ships, they and thousands of others were marched from the docks and auctioned off to their new masters and employers.

FELONIOUS FEMALES

American archives of 1640 record that 'Goody Gregory of Springfield, being grievously angered by a neighbour, abused her profanely, saying, "Before God, I could break your head!" She acknowledged her "great sine and fault" like a woman, but she paid her fine and sat with her legs locked in the stocks like a man, since she swore like one!'

No block was used in an execution by the sword. Anne Boleyn was beheaded while kneeling upright.

In Roman society, prostitutes were reviled but nevertheless still visited in their refuges, the low arches which covered the dark areas bordering the sides of the large houses. These arched pits were called *fornices*, the origin of the English word 'fornication'.

By an Act passed during the reign of James I, 'lewd women were to be committed to the house of correction (a prison designed to correct their way of life), there set to labour for the term of one whole year; but the woman is not to be apprehended till the child be born, and she has recovered her strength.'

Ale-wives who sold bad ale had to sit on a 'Cucking Stool' outside their houses, to be jeered at by their neighbours.

A woman in seventeenth-century Virginia, America, was found guilty of slander. Unfortunately there was no ducking stool available, so 'she was sentenced to be drawen ouer the Kings Creeke at the sterne of a boate or Canoux, also the next Saboth day in the time of [i.e., during] Diuine seruise to appear before the minister and congregation to admit her sins and beg forgiveness.'

In Edward III's reign, distinguishing 'ladies of the town' from 'good and noble dames' was such a problem that a regulation was promulgated stating: 'Whereas the common lewd women which dwell in the city have assumed the fashion of being clad in the manner of good and noble dames, in unreasonable manner, it is ordered that no such lewd women shall be so daring as to be attired in any vesture trimmed with fur such as miniver [white fur], poppelle of squirrel or any other manner of noble bulge [?]. But let every such lewd woman go openly with a hood of cloth, so that all folks, natives and strangers, may have knowledge of what rank they are.'

In the fourteenth century, Elizabeth Moring, 'under colour of the craft of broidery, which she pretended to follow, incited women who were with her, to live a lewd life and consort with friars, chaplains and all other such men. She was banished from the City of London.'

German women convicted of infanticide were, until late in the sixteenth century, sentenced to death by drowning, the assistant executioner holding them under the water by means of a long pole.

At her trial in 1721, Mary Andrews refused to plead guilty or not guilty, and it was not until three cords had been bound round her thumbs and tightened until they snapped that she finally submitted a plea.

Seventeenth-century brothel keepers in Southwark, London, were forbidden to employ 'any woman of religion, or any man's wife';

nor was 'any single woman, who would leave her sin, to be kept against her will'.

Under Edward I a London bye-law stipulated that 'No woman of the City shall go to market or on the King's Highway without a hood furred with other than lambskin or rabbit skin, on pain of losing her hood to the sheriffs, save only those ladies who wear fur capes; because regatresses [retailers], nurses and women of loose life bedizen [adorn] themselves with miniver in guise of good ladies.'

In the 1660s the judicial penalty for many offences in England was to be publicly whipped. One law stated that 'launderers and laundresses who dare wash unclean Linen or throw out the water or suds or fowle clothes in the open streetes, or who took pay for washing for a soldier or laborer, or who gave old torn linen for good linen' should be severely whipped. Other offences carrying the same penalty were the slitting or cutting off the ends of hogs' ears in order to remove the marks which gave proof of ownership; stealing tobacco; running away from home; drunkenness; and removal of land boundaries.

The sentence passed on Sarah Swarton in February 1618 was that 'she be whipped to Westminster, and after, from the same place to Cheapside; there to be branded with F.A., signifying false accusation of a neighbour, one letter on each cheek; to return back again to the Fleet prison, there to remain till they be weary of her, and then sent back to Bridewell [corrective institution], there to spend and end her days.'

Women who persisted in quarrelling with each other in medieval France were sentenced to wear a Double-Scolds' Collar for a prescribed length of time. This was a one-piece lockable wooden collar with holes in it to accommodate the wrists and necks of the two antagonists – facing each other!

For real ingenuity in picking pockets, credit must be given to Mary Young, alias Jenny Diver. She had a pair of false arms sculptured which she inserted in the sleeves of her dress, positioning the hands together in her lap when she was seated in church or at a theatre. She would then slide her hands out of slits in the sides of the garment and extract valuables from the pockets or handbags of those sitting on each side of her. Her long and profitable career came to an end on 18 March 1740 on Tyburn's scaffold, where her real hands were tied but the hangman's weren't.

Perhaps one of the most horrific methods of judicial execution was that carried out in fifteenth-century France, when a female thief named Perette was sentenced 'to be buried alive before the gallows'.

In 1954 New Zealanders were shocked at the brutal murder of Mrs Honora Parker, but their reaction turned to one of horrified disbelief when it emerged that the crime had been committed by her sixteen-year-old daughter Pauline and Pauline's closest friend, fifteen-year-old Juliet Hulme. Mrs Parker had discovered that the two girls had formed a lesbian relationship and so was relieved when Mr Hulme announced that his family would be moving to South Africa. Pauline Parker was determined to accompany them and, when her mother declared her opposition, the two girls deliberately murdered her, striking her 47 times with a brick. Both were found guilty and imprisoned 'during Her Majesty's Pleasure' but were released four years later. They no doubt still retained their consciences.

Between 1900 and 1948, 936 women were committed for trial in this country; 126 were sentenced to death, but only 11 of them hanged.

Marianne Bachmeier was nicknamed the 'Avenging Mother' by the press when, in March 1981, she walked across the courtroom in Lubeck, Germany, and fired seven bullets into Klaus Grabowski, who was being tried for the sexual murder of Marianne's seven-year-old daughter Anna. Making no attempt to escape, she was arrested and, having gained much public sympathy and support, was later sentenced to six years in jail for manslaughter.

The only woman executed in England because of her political opinions was Lady Margaret Bulmer, who refused to acknowledge Henry VIII's supremacy and opposed the dissolution of the monasteries, and was burned at the stake at Smithfield on 25 May 1537.

Fourteenth-century taverns were identified by signs, such as The Swan or The Bell, hanging outside their establishments. Prostitutes used similar signs to attract clients, but theirs were not suspended from brackets but painted on the wall.

Unless they confessed their sinful ways, prostitutes in the fourteenth century were denied a Christian burial and were interred outside the cemetery in an area known as the 'Single Women's Churchyard'.

NOOSE-KNOTTERS AND SLICERS

Few hangmen achieved any social recognition, but one went on to attain the highest position in the land: the sheriff and hangman in Eire County, New York, was Grover Cleveland, who became President of the United States not once but twice.

French executioner Henri Sanson, deep in debt, pledged the guillotine in return for a cash loan. A few weeks later the Public Prosecutor ordered him to prepare the machine for an execution. When Sanson admitted he hadn't got it, he was fired!

After beheading the Chevalier de la Barre with the sword, French executioner Charles-Henri Sanson, on seeing the victim still upright but swaying gently, is reported to have exclaimed 'Shake yourself – it is done!'

Nineteenth-century Australian hangmen disguised themselves from vengeful friends of their victims, some by wearing masks, others with full black beards, held in place by tapes tied at the back of the head, and matching false bushy eyebrows. All wore thick leather gloves, high boots, long black coats and wide-brimmed black slouch hats.

So efficient was the French executioner Charles-Henri Sanson when operating the Paris guillotine during the Revolution that at one time he and his team beheaded no fewer than twelve men and women in thirteen minutes, 21 in 43 minutes and three hundred in three days. These record times included escorting each bound victim from the waiting queue up the scaffold steps, securing them to the machine and removing the torsos after decapitation.

English hangman John Ellis executed 203 victims during his term of office. He committed suicide in 1929 by cutting his throat.

When Australia was used as a penal colony for English convicts, the executioner in New South Wales, an ex-con named Alexander Green, hanged 490 felons during his thirty years' reign on the scaffold. He was committed to a lunatic asylum in 1855.

Few condemned men fought on the way to the scaffold as fiercely as murderer William Henry Palmer in 1912; it took ten prison officers, struggling frantically, to subdue him. So violently did he behave on arrival at the trapdoors that hangman Ellis decided not to tie his ankles; instead, he rapidly capped and noosed the frenzied man and pulled the lever, afterwards swearing that it was the most terrifying execution he had ever had to perform.

During the French Revolution the scaffold was railed round after an executioner fell from it and was fatally injured.

Sentenced to death for the murder of her husband in 1922, Edith Thompson collapsed completely in the condemned cell and had to be carried, limp and inert, to the scaffold by four warders, a task made more difficult by the narrowness of the prison doorways. On the drop she was held upright by the men while executioner Ellis slipped the white hood and noose over her head and operated the lever; oblivious of her fate, she plunged into the pit, dying instantly and without a struggle.

Franz Schmidt, Nuremberg's executioner from 1578 to 1617, executed at least 361 criminals and administered minor punishments to 345 others.

The type of crane known as a derrick was so called after an English hangman of the same name, because it resembled a gibbet from which the bodies of executed felons were suspended.

At the time of the French Revolution the executioner in the capital was known as Monsieur de Paris.

Hangmen of any nationality welcomed a victim who prayed on the scaffold, since it indicated that he had resigned himself to his fate and so was unlikely to resist being noosed.

Like some of their English counterparts, German hangmen occasionally broke the law and paid the price. In 1479 executioner Hans committed treason – and was beheaded by his own deputy.

The ex-convict hangman Alexander Green, transported to Australia in 1824, hanged eight felons in one day in 1828. The number included one woman, Florence Driscoll, convicted of sheep-stealing.

In 1535 German hangman Gilg, ordered to execute, by drowning, a woman guilty of infanticide, took advantage of a clause in the judicial regulations and saved her from such a terrible death by marrying her.

A letter T was chalked across the division of the two hinged trapdoors of twentieth-century scaffolds, so that when the victim's feet were positioned each side of the letter's upright, they were directly over the gap between the doors.

A Royal Commission of 1949–53 debated whether hanging should be replaced by some other method. Many alternatives were considered but, although death by lethal injection appeared to be more humane, it was rejected on medical advice, and the rope held sway (!).

In the diary of executioner Franz Schmidt, against the date 26 October 1581, he records that 'Michael Passelt, who was wedded both to his mistress and her daughter, had long lived in lecherous intimacy with them. I beheaded him here in Nuremberg; his body afterwards was burnt.'

Despite being only too aware of the penalty for murder, English executioner John Price killed a woman and in 1718 was duly hanged.

Edwin Davis, American executioner in the early 1900s, always checked the power circuitry of the electric chair by inserting the electrodes into a joint of beef, switching the current on and making sure the meat sizzled.

It was the length of the hangman's rope that determined the manner of the victim's death; if too short, he or she slowly suffocated and died by strangulation; if too long, the victim's head was torn off.

Not every executioner was exclusively mercenary: so patriotic was Egyptian hangman Ashmawi that when he hanged a notorious spy, Awad Mikhail, in 1953, he waived his usual fee of £5 and did it for free.

After a hanging, a piece of the rope used would, it was believed, not only cure aches and pains but also act as a lucky charm. The application of the 'death sweat' from the hand of a slowly swinging corpse on the gallows was also deemed efficacious as a remedy for scrofulous diseases, and this practice was permitted until as late as 1760.

The German executioner Franz Schmidt did not flinch from his duty when his brother-in-law Frederick Werner was found guilty of murder in 1585; after nipping his flesh twice with a pair of hot pincers, Franz secured him to the horizontally mounted wheel and proceeded methodically to shatter his limbs, taking 31 blows with an iron bar to do so.

Some condemned men were made to wear their full-length shrouds on the scaffold in order to prevent them, should they manage to free their bound hands, from attempting to remove the noose.

Scottish hangmen were known as 'doomsters' or 'deemsters'.

In the nineteenth century the first four verses of the 51st Psalm were known as the 'neck verse' and were sung by the spectators crowded around the scaffold.

The Tyburn execution site in London is indicated by a brass plate on a traffic island near Marble Arch. Care must be taken on crossing the busy road to approach it, lest another tombstone should bear the inscription 'Died at Tyburn'!

So skilled with the execution sword was German Johann Michel Widman (1665–1736) that on one occasion he not only neatly decapitated his victim but nearly severed the hands of his assistant who was supporting the man.

Until capital punishment was abolished in the last century, the official appointed by law to carry out an execution in England was the Sheriff, who, if he were unable to employ a hangman, would have to perform the deed himself.

In ancient Rome, criminals sentenced to death were secured in a sack which also contained a viper, a dog, a monkey and a cock; the sack was then dropped into the nearest river or lake.

Public hangings took place on 'Wryneck Day', so called because the victims' heads were tilted to one side by the noose.

Following World War II, those Nazis condemned to die after their trial at Nuremberg were hanged. Ten of the most prominent were despatched by the American John C. Woods, who, during his career as an executioner, hanged a total of 347 criminals.

Pierre Lacenaire killed a woman and her son in Paris in December 1834, but the price he paid was truly horrific for, as he lay strapped to the guillotine, the blade rapidly descended – only to stop, some say, with the razor-sharp edge of the blade actually touching the back of his neck! The machine had probably been left out in the rain, causing the wooden uprights to expand. The executioner had to hoist the blade to the top and release it again, whereupon the head of Lacenaire dropped into the waiting basket.

On 16 February 1568 the Spanish rulers of the Netherlands decreed that all the inhabitants would suffer the fate of heretics: they would be put to death. Executions on such a large scale were obviously impossible; nevertheless, eight hundred residents were hanged or burned at the stake during the first week, and many others executed later.

Even before the French Revolution, many towns had their own executioners, more than 160 of such gentlemen being equipped with the beheading sword.

Further to unnerve the doomed aristocrats awaiting their turn to be guillotined in 1796, French executioner Hentz sadistically arranged 25 previously severed heads in the form of a flower-bed in front of the scaffold.

Chinese execution by the sword in the nineteenth century conformed to a precise and formal ceremony. On one occasion in 1851, 33 victims knelt, heads stretched forward, in rows. The executioner approached each victim at a right angle, positioned the long, slightly curved sword-blade a few inches above the man's neck, shouted a warning to him to keep still, raised the weapon head-high and brought it down with all his strength, then moved on to the next victim. So accurate were his actions that all 33 crouching figures were beheaded in less than three minutes. At one side an assistant dipped a bunch of short lengths of rushes into the streams of blood and dropped them into a large pot; the blood-soaked rushes were apparently much sought after for medicinal purposes.

French executioner Henri Desfourneaux took over the scaffold in 1939 and guillotined nearly one thousand five hundred men and women during the next twelve years, many of them war criminals.

French executioner Denis suffered for his lack of expertise when, in February 1488, he attempted to execute a coiner, Loys Secretain. After first binding his victim's arms and legs, he threw him into the cauldron to be boiled prior to being drawn and hanged, but the cords slackened and, despite Denis holding him under, 'using a great iron hook', Loys kept rising to the surface. The spectators decided that this was obviously an Act of God and attacked the executioner so severely that he died of his wounds. In the rioting, Loys made himself scarce!

Eighteenth-century criminals delicately referred to the physical result of being hanged as 'having a dry mouth and a pissen pair of breeches'.

Thailand's executioner until 1984 was Pathom Kruapeng, who despatched his seated victims by firing a rifle which was fixed to a stand about twenty feet away, its muzzle protruding through a hole in a screen. Kruapeng, unable to see the target, would continue firing until told that the victim was dead, sometimes requring as many as five bullets or more.

Executioners throughout the world have almost invariably been denigrated and despised by society in general. In Spain the executioner received his fee from a priest, who threw it to him from some distance away. Even the hangman's donkey, on which he transported the felon and the coffin to the scaffold, was an outcast, the animal having its ears cropped so that no one would accidentally use it for any other purpose.

Because there were more victims than the guillotine could cope with, Revolutionary Representative Carrier had them herded on to barges moored in the river, which were then sunk. He called it 'vertical deportation'.

In the 1794 uprising in the Vendée the revolutionary Mayor of Angers wrote to his colleague in Paris: 'Our holy mother guillotine works; in three days she has shaven eleven monks, one former nun, a general and a superb Englishman, six feet tall, whose head was de trop. It is in the sack today.'

A Corinthian warlord named Sinnis was given the nickname of 'Pine Bender' because of the way in which he exterminated his enemies. Having ordered his men to bend two adjacent young trees towards the ground and tie the tops of them together with rope, he would then have them secure each of an opponent's ankles to each of the trees. A swift severance of the rope with a knife allowed the trees to straighten up rapidly, with inevitable and ghastly results.

The knot of the noose was positioned under the left ear for no other reason than that the hangman, who was usually right-handed, held the slip-knot of the noose in his right hand as he dropped the noose over the condemned person's head.

A Macabre Miscellany

In bygone prison record books, the annotation 'sus. per col.' was entered against the name of a prisoner who had been hanged by the neck, the term being an abbreviation for *suspensus per collum*.

When the executioner and his victim, Bailly, ex-mayor of Paris, reached the guillotine scaffold in 1793, it was discovered that some planks were missing, so the tumbril had to return and collect the timber; but on the return journey the boards took up so much space in the transport that the victim and executioner had to walk alongside!

Among the Israelites the man who won a legal case personally carried out the sentence passed on the other party. If the 'loser' had been found guilty of murder and condemned to death, members of the victim's family and others employed by the court 'would contend for the honour of carrying out that duty, because those who released society from its scourges were regarded as its benefactors'.

At Carpentras, during the Revolution, French executioner Berger had to work single-handedly. On one occasion, having earlier drunk twelve francs' worth of brandy, he guillotined a particularly well-built victim, then backed the tumbril up to the scaffold to collect the remains. Unfortunately he found he hadn't reversed the cart close enough, so he tied the headless corpse to the back of the cart and dragged it to the cemetery, duly earning himself a prison sentence.

One of the perks claimed by eighteenth-century French executioners was being the town's knacker; they had the privilege of skinning any dead beasts, usually horses or cattle, found around town, and selling the pelts and flesh.

Orders were issued in 1796 that all French executioners should clean the guillotine after use and catch the blood in a barrel rather than let it drip on to the ground, 'otherwise the blood of the aristocrats flowing from them would infect the air that every republican must breathe.' For the same reason, the baskets used to convey the decapitated corpses to the cemeteries had to be lined with oil cloth.

Edwin Davis, the New York executioner, despatched 240 criminals, including seven in one day, until retiring in 1914; his successor, John Hulbert, executed 140 during the next thirteen years.

During the execution of Lord Ferrers in 1760 for the murder of his steward, the sheriffs and other officials present at the Tyburn hanging sat at a table on the scaffold and ate their breakfast, while the body swung beside them until the regulation hour had elapsed.

In order to reduce the suffering caused to a victim by a slipping noose while being hanged, a Dr J. Marshall devised a 'chin trough' to hold the rope in position. To put this to the test he asked the various surgical schools in London to 'lend' him some of the corpses they were using for instruction, promising to return them unspoiled so that students could continue dissecting them. Alas, they demurred, and the device was never adopted.

When executing by the sword, European executioners, wielding it in both hands, allowed the severed heads to fall and roll across the scaffold boards, but their Japanese counterparts were skilled in daki-kubi, slicing through the neck so precisely that a shred of skin remained, connecting the head to the torso, which was subsequently cut with a knife.

The public hangman of Victoria, Australia, committed suicide in 1924, as did New York's executioner John Hulbert in 1929.

A MACABRE MISCELLANY

Austrian executioner Johann Lang committed suicide in 1938, as did his fellow practitioner, Paul Späthe of Cologne, who first lit one candle for each of his victims – then did away with himself.

In criminal jargon, a 'Hempen Widow' was a woman whose husband had been hanged.

The traditional name for English hangmen of 'Jack Ketch' is believed to have originated with that of Richard Jacquett, the owner of the area of Tyburn in which the gallows was originally situated.

The procedure for swearing in an executioner in the eighteenth century involved the candidate having to appear before London's city fathers. Standing in front of a table on which was laid out his official tool-kit of fetters, handcuffs, scourges and, of course, ropes, he would then have to take an oath on the Bible that he would execute all those condemned by the courts 'without favouring father and mother or brother or sister or any friend whatsoever, so help me God'.

PUNISHMENT TOOL-KITS

The 'Nuremberg Maiden' was a hollow, spike-lined figure into which the victim was thrust, the door, similarly lined, then being closed.

A 'Drunkard's Cloak' was a barrel with holes in it for arms and head, worn as a punishment by drunkards.

A 'Scold's Bridle', also called a 'Brank', was a cage locked around a nagging woman's head, incorporating an iron plate which held her tongue down. Wearing it, she would be paraded around town by the Beadle, with a bell on a spring, mounted atop the Bridle, announcing her approach to residents.

The 'Scavenger's Daughter' in the Tower of London was a hinged torture instrument which was tightened to compress a kneeling victim until eventually blood was exuded from bodily orifices.

Indiana's electric chair was so antiquated that in October 1985 it required three surges of current, and William Vandiver did not die until seventeen minutes had elapsed.

If you were 'married to the Duke of Exeter's Daughter' you were being tortured on the rack, the device having been introduced into the Tower of London by that nobleman.

A *knout* is a Russian type of wooden-handled whip, having a lash 36 inches in length, which was used to punish both men and women.

A MACABRE MISCELLANY

Not for nothing was London called 'The City of Gallows' in the eighteenth century, for the grim structures stood at Tyburn, Kennington Common, Fleet Street, the Strand, the Haymarket and Bow Street, Old Street and Finsbury. And when rioting broke out in 1780, portable gallows were used, rioters being hanged on the spot.

German torture methods in the sixteenth century included one known as the *Kranz* or *Schneiden*, which consisted of a strap positioned around the victim's head and then slowly tightened.

The 'Pendulum' torture consisted of a large curved blade which swung from side to side and slowly descended closer and closer to the midriff of a prone and tightly bound victim until –

Apega of Sparta was a mechanical figure, mounted on small wheels, which slowly advanced and hugged its victim, spikes hidden beneath its robes bringing about a hideous death.

The *Falterkammer* is a German torture chamber.

'Pyrewinkes' were fifteenth-century Scottish thumbscrews.

Offenders sentenced to the 'Jougs' were chained to the village cross or whipping post by an iron collar around the neck.

The French punishment *Tenaillement* involved hot wax or lead poured into the victim's open wounds.

The 'Spanish Chair' was made of iron; the victim was secured in it and a fire lit beneath it to induce confessions.

The torture in which a drop of water was allowed to fall on the bound victim's forehead repeatedly until he either confessed or went mad was devised by a sixteenth-century lawyer named Hippolytus de Marsilis.

In the *Tormento de Toca* torture, water was poured down a victim's throat through gauze, eventually forcing the material into his stomach.

Among the atrocities inflicted on the Armenians in 1915–16 by the Turks was the *Bastinado* punishment: being caned on the soles of the feet.

In the city of St Petersburg, Russia, some eighteenth-century criminals were marked for life by having their nostrils slit; others were branded by having their skin punctured and black powder rubbed into the wounds.

The guillotine was also used in Florence, Italy, around the year 1778, for serious crimes. Other criminals were hanged, then buried in the clothes they were wearing, coffins not being permitted.

The Pillory was an upright post, at the top of which were fixed two horizontal boards, hinged together at one end, the other end having locking facilities. Both had matching half-holes, one large one to accommodate the victim's neck, two smaller holes for the wrists, these being so positioned as to prevent the victim from protecting his or her face. In 1648 John Geere of Maryland, guilty of perjury, 'was nayled by both eares in the pillory, three nailes in each eare, and the eares to be slitt out after, and whipped twenty good lashes.'

When rifles are handed out to a firing squad, one of them used to be loaded with a blank round as a salve for members' consciences. However, twentieth-century and later weapons, when firing blanks, do not kick as they do when firing live rounds, and the barrels are cooler – so any twinges of conscience have to be endured or ignored.

To prevent sympathisers from climbing up and retrieving the corpse of Adam Graham, hanged for murder in 1747 and encased in a suit of iron strips riveted tightly around the body, the Carlisle authorities made the gibbet post twelve yards high – and drove twelve thousand nails, porcupine-like, into it!

The 'Scottish Maiden', based on the Halifax Gibbet, was also a forerunner of the French guillotine and decapitated at least 120 victims; it was last used in 1710.

The Halifax Gibbet in Yorkshire was the forerunner of the guillotine by more than two hundred years. Used in the late fifteenth and early sixteenth centuries, it consisted of a heavy blade which, having been hauled to the top by a pulley, travelled rapidly downwards between two wooden uprights to sever the head of the felon kneeling between them. There was no executioner: the blade was held in place by a pin, the rope attached to it was stretched out and gripped by as many members of the crowd as possible, and they decided, by pulling it, whether the felon should be executed. Since it took more than one person to release the pin, that would seem to have been a genuinely democratic decision. The Halifax Gibbet was used to despatch 49 men and women.

Offenders in Czarist Russia were beaten with a *pleti*, a wooden whip with small lead balls on the extremities of its three thongs.

Boston citizens who flagrantly disregarded the Sabbath were sentenced to be punished at the whipping post. In 1643 Roger Scott, 'for repeated sleeping on the Lord's Day and for striking the person who waked him from his godless slumbers', was sentenced to be severely whipped.

Among nicknames given to the guillotine during the French Revolution were the 'Patriotic Shortener', the 'National Razor' and the 'Widow Maker'.

In fifteenth century Greece, one devastating torture involved the victim's feet being bathed with salt water, after which goats were allowed to lick them.

The phrase 'Hold your tongue' could well have been derived from a painful punishment inflicted on the early settlers in America. The records of the Massachusetts Bay Colony report that: '6 September, Boston, 1636; Robert Shorthouse for swearing by the bloud of God was sentenced to have his tongue put into a cleft stick, and soe stand for halfe an houre, & Elizabeth wife of Thomas Applegate was censured to stand with her tongue in a cleft stick for halfe an houre for swearinge, railing and reviling.'

In earlier centuries, some European villages had their own punishments, among these being the Malefactor's Collar Pillory, a wide wooden collar which also incorporated holes for the hands; locked in position around the culprit's neck and wrists, it had to be worn in public for the prescribed number of hours.

Possibly used during the Spanish Inquisition, the Spanish Mouth-Pear was an iron pear-shaped instrument which was forced into the victim's mouth; when a button was pressed, its two segments would spring apart, extending the victim's jaws and so effectively keeping him or her silent.

In the 1930s the Californian authorities invited San Francisco journalists to watch the newly introduced gas chamber in action, using live pigs. The method failed to receive a good write-up: some reporters condemned it as worse than being hanged, drawn and quartered.

The execution axe held in the Tower of London, believed to have been last used in 1747 during the Scottish Rebellion, is approximately 36 inches long and weighs 17lbs 15oz. The blade is 16 inches long with a cutting edge of 10 inches. Unlike a sword, it did not cut, but crushed its way through bone and muscle, sinew and flesh.

Having been sentenced to a number of hours standing in the pillory, one culprit stood on the footboard, only to have it collapse under his weight. Even in the nineteenth century, people knew their rights, so he sued the council – and won!

The French guillotine was often jokingly referred to as *la bécane*, a phrase applied to old shunting engines, because of the rumbling noise the blade made in its descent.

Execution swords used by German executioners in the seventeenth century were superb examples of the weapon maker's craft. Their lengths varied from 30 to over 40 inches, and they weighed about 4lbs. Each blade was 2½ins wide and had a 'fuller', a full-length longitudinal groove on each side to allow the blood to flow away from the razor-sharp cutting edges, and the two-handed grip was covered with non-slip fish scales. The tip was rounded, a sharp point being unnecessary. Execution swords were usually inscribed with an appropriate motto such as 'Wan Ich Dass Schwert thue aufheben, So Wunsche Ich dem suncler das E. leben' – 'Whenever I raise the sword, I wish the sinner an everlasting life', or 'Die Herren Steuren Dem Unheill, Ich Execuirire Iht Ends Urtheill' – 'The judges check evil, I carry out their capital punishment.'

Three terrifying sounds reverberated around town squares during the French Revolution: the thud as the *bascule*, the plank to which the victim had been secured, fell into place, bringing the victim's head into position below the pendant blade; the clang as the *lunette*, the iron collar, dropped around his neck to hold him immoveable; and the fearful rumbling of the blade as it descended at ever-increasing speed.

A favoured few of those about to be burned at the stake were allowed to have small bags of gunpowder tied under their arms and between their legs, to shorten their suffering as the flames rose higher.

When, in the nineteenth century, the great debate continued in the USA regarding which electric current should be used nation-wide, AC (Alternating Current) or DC (Direct Current), the company advocating DC toured the country and demonstrated the inherent dangers of AC by employing it to electrocute various animals, including a cat, a dog and even a horse.

WHAT A WAY TO GO!

In order to commit suicide, young student Kiyoko Matsumoto jumped into the open mouth of an active volcano on the Japanese island of Amami-O-Shima in 1933.

In both World Wars enemy spies were executed by firing squad within the Tower of London.

In eighteenth-century Sweden, women sentenced to death were beheaded by the axe; the scaffold was then set on fire at its four corners and consumed with the body.

James, Duke of Monmouth, attempted to overthrow King James II but his peasant army was defeated and the Duke, though pleading for mercy, was beheaded on 15 July 1685; no fewer than five blows with the axe were necessary.

American newsreader Christine Hubbock committed suicide in 1970 in the most public manner possible: she shot herself while in the middle of a programme.

During the reign of Peter the Great, mutinous Russian soldiers were dealt with expeditiously by their master; they were forced to kneel over a log, then he would move along the line, beheading them personally, one at a time.

Australia's 'man they couldn't hang' was murderer Joseph

48

Samuels, who, in the 1880s, was duly noosed on the Sydney gallows, but, when the trapdoors opened, the rope snapped halfway along its length and Samuels fell into the pit. He was brought up on to the scaffold and re-roped and again the drop was operated, but this time the rope snapped at the overhead beam. Again the man was escorted up the steps to the platform and again the noose was positioned – only for it to snap near his neck! With the crowd now threatening to rush the scaffold, the Governor was summoned, and without further ado he pardoned the half-strangled, half-fainting victim.

In ancient Sicily the 'Brazen Bull' was a life-size hollow brass effigy; the victim was secured inside, and a fire lighted beneath it.

The 'Catherine Wheel' firework was named after St Catherine, who was sentenced to death by being tied to the outer rim of a wheel, which was then rolled over spikes.

In some states of the USA felons were hanged by being jerked violently upwards by means of an appropriately weighted mechanism, instead of the traditional method of dropping through a hatch.

In 1688 John Stansfield cursed his father, then murdered him. His sentence was that he be hanged till he was dead, his tongue be cut out and burned on the scaffold and his corpse be hanged in chains. Nor was that all, for his name, fame, memory and honours were ordered to be extinct, and his coat of arms to be deleted from the Scottish Book of Arms.

Just one blow of the axe was necessary to behead Lady Jane Grey.

There was no thought of commuting William Taylor's death sentence when, in 1893, the routine second charge of two thousand volts surged through him but nothing happened. Instead, the badly burned and unconscious man was carried into an adjoining room and given morphine and chloroform to keep him alive. Meanwhile the technicians worked desperately until the fault was rectified; then, still unconscious, he was carried back to the chair, strapped down, and electrocuted.

In the early 1900s Austrian criminals were executed by strangulation: the hangman not only tightened the noose around the victim's neck but squeezed his throat at the same time.

François Damiens, would-be assassin of France's Louis XV, was first hideously tortured, then spread-eagled and torn apart by four young horses.

A convict in the 1930s who saw the body of a fellow inmate immediately after the man's execution described how 'his neck was wrenched into a grotesque shape, his face black with extravasated blood, and his dead eyeballs protruded in a fixed and glassy stare'.

Aaron Mitchell died slowly in a Californian gas chamber in 1976, staring fixedly at the officials through the glass window, gasping for breath and with saliva trickling down his chin. It took nearly fifteen minutes for his heart to stop beating.

While Ray Landry was being prepared for execution by lethal injection in 1988, the tube through which the drugs were passing into one of his veins suddenly ruptured. The delay while it was replaced by a serviceable one resulted in the unconscious man not finally succumbing until 24 minutes later.

Between AD 994 and 1035 Greek felons were first skinned alive, then their bodies were impaled on spikes until death brought an end to their suffering.

Pirates were executed at Wapping in London in the sixteenth century by being hanged, then left suspended in the Thames for three high tides, before being gibbeted.

A Spanish method of execution employed even into the 1900s was garrotting the felon. The seated victim was bound to a post immediately behind him and a metal strap was positioned around his throat, the ends of which passed through a hole in the post. By means of a screw mechanism, the strap could be slowly tightened. A more modern variation incorporates two metal bands and a lever at the back of the post pulling one band back and the other forward, thereby dislocating the spinal column and rendering the victim unconscious and, hopefully, dead within seconds.

The usual method of execution for unpremeditated murder in eighteenth-century Holland was beheading by the sword. However, should the murder have been premeditated, the criminal was secured to a cross laid flat on the scaffold and his limbs systematically shattered with an iron bar; the *coup de grâce* was a blow to the heart.

To test the efficiency of the gas chamber in 1924 the prison authorities put two cats in it, closed the door and started to pump the gas in. Watching closely they saw the animals eventually stagger, then collapse – upon which they proceeded with the planned execution.

The first railway fatality in England occurred in September 1830 during the opening of the Manchester to Liverpool line, the unfortunate man being William Huskisson MP, who was standing on the track with three others when a train approached. Though warned by a shout, Huskisson, old and in ill-health, hesitated and was struck by the engine 'which dashed like a thunderbolt upon him and passed over his leg, smashing and mangling it in a most horrible way.' Despite medical aid, he died the same day.

On the orders of Oliver Cromwell, Royalist supporter James Graham, Marquis of Montrose, was hanged on a thirty-foot gallows, 'then his head was strucken off and spiked on Edinburgh Towlebooth, and his armes and legge were hanged upp in other publique townes, and his body buried at the common burying-place.'

The 'Paddington Frisk' was the bizarre name given to the 'dance' of the struggling being hanged at Tyburn – which is in the parish of Paddington.

Death by firing squad isn't always instantaneous. In Zante prison, Turkey, in 1783, a notorious pirate was sentenced to death; no fewer than three volleys were fired, none of them fatal, and he was despatched by a pistol-shot to the ear. He was then decapitated, his head being mounted on a pole.

When, on 23 May 1934, the legendary outlaws Bonnie and Clyde, Bonnie Parker and Clyde Barrow, were finally cornered by the police after their murderous travels across the States, they must have thought that they were invulnerable and escape would be easy, for in the car they had an arsenal of three rifles, twelve pistols, two pump-action shotguns and two thousand rounds of ammunition. But even as they attempted to open the car door a veritable fusillade of shots rang out as over five hundred rounds from the guns of the police marksmen punctured the car like a sieve. The firing continued for nearly four minutes. The bullet-riddled cadavers were then taken to a morgue in the nearby town, where queues of morbidly minded spectators paid a dollar each to view the grisly remains.

George Joseph Smith killed each of his three wives in the early 1900s while they were having a bath; gripping them by the ankles, he lifted their legs up high, making it impossible for them to raise themselves above the water level and so causing death by drowning. Initially he claimed that they had fainted while bathing, but justice prevailed and he was later hanged.

Opposing the then president of Equatorial Guinea in June 1974 was politically inadvisable: those who disagreed with his views were drenched in petrol and set alight.

There can be few families as murderous as Mrs Barker and her four boys, who, in the 1930s, spent their time robbing banks and killing anyone who got in their way, their score eventually reaching at least ten victims. When they were caught, Arthur got life in Alcatraz, where he was shot dead in 1936 during an escape bid; Herman killed a police officer, then committed suicide; and brother Lloyd served 25 years in prison – only to be killed by his wife two years later! As for the matriarch, Kate, she and Fred were cornered by FBI agents in Florida and died in a hail of bullets.

The Roman emperor Nero devised a method of execution whereby the victim had to dig a deep grave, in the bottom of which a sharp stake was imbedded, protruding upwards. The victim was then bound and thrown in, to be impaled on the stake; after which the grave was filled in.

During a deadly sixteenth-century epidemic which killed a third of the European population, great pits were dug in churchyards 'filled to overflowing, wherein the bodies were laid by the hundred as they arrived. In these pits they were packed in layers, as goods are stowed in a ship, and each layer covered with a little earth, until they mounted to the top.'

Seventeenth-century London parishes employed 'Searchers' to record the causes of deaths occurring in the district. Their records include such exotically named diseases as 'Flox and Small Pox, French pox, Grief, Griping of the Guts, Kings-evil, Stopping of the Stomach, Surfeit, Teeth, Wind, Worms, and Tissick' (this last being a misspelling of 'phthisic', consumption).

John Foxe in his *Book of Martyrs* recorded how Joan Clerk, daughter of William Tylsworth, was forced to set fire to her father, who was burned at the stake as a heretic; her husband William Clerk had to bring wood for fuel.

Edward II was murdered by 'the insertion of a red-hot iron in his fundament' in Berkeley Castle in 1327.

The Tartars had a law whereby, when a man died, his nearest relative was buried with him; the Chinese mandarins were accompanied into the next world by their concubines and slaves, who were buried alive.

Despite all attempts by the British Government to discourage the Indian rite of suttee, whereby the widow voluntarily burns herself to death on the funeral pyre of her dead husband, a total of 5,997 women sacrificed themselves in this manner during the period 1815–25.

Many criminals are executed by passing electricity through them, but the officials subjected American murderer Henry McCracken to the same sort of treatment in order to bring him to his senses – then they executed him by other means! McCracken's mental state had deteriorated to the extent that he was no longer thinking logically or rationally, and prison psychiatrists agreed that so total was his mental collapse, it was unacceptable under the law to execute him. Accordingly McCracken was subjected to electro-convulsive therapy and as soon as signs of sanity were seen to return, was promptly escorted to the gas chamber.

A group of children from well-to-do families living in Rennes during the French Revolution were called 'the Hope of our Country' and, in order to involve them in the class struggle, were encouraged to shoot those unfortunates who had been arrested by the local militia. Batches of fifteen or twenty victims at a time were made the targets, but most of them, owing to the inaccuracy of the youngsters, were only injured by the first salvo of shots.

Much American media coverage was given to the many sadistic murders committed by Albert DeSalvo, the 'Boston Strangler', in 1964. Despite public demand for the death sentence, he was eventually given a life sentence in prison. He might have escaped execution, but he couldn't escape a knife accurately wielded by a fellow prisoner, seven years later.

John Bradby, a fifteenth-century heretic, was rolled to the stake in an empty beer barrel and set on fire; he was then freed and offered a pension of 3d. a day if he recanted. He didn't, so was rebarrelled and burned to death.

Following the revolution in Romania in 1989, President Nicolae Ceaucescu and his wife Elena were killed by firing squad, the members of which were either so trigger-happy or so ill-disciplined that they started firing their machine guns before being ordered, and many others present were injured.

John Bunting and Robert Wagner were jailed for life in 2003 in Adelaide, guilty of one of Australia's worst serial killings. Eight bodies were discovered in acid-filled barrels in Snowtown, ninety miles north of the city, and others were found buried; all had been tortured.

When a clown from Cooke's Equestrian Circus crossed the river in a tub drawn by four geese at Yarmouth in May 1825, the suspension bridge was so crowded with spectators that it collapsed, killing more than a hundred people.

Eighty-five murders were committed by Bruno Ludke in Germany between 1928 and 1943, crimes accompanied by rape and robbery. Instead of putting him on public trial, the Nazi authorities used him as a medical guinea-pig and, after performing some experimental surgery, executed him by means of a fatal injection in April 1944.

When a fire broke out at the southern end of London Bridge in 1282, people rushed across to help those fighting the blaze, but the southerly wind then blew the flames to the City end, trapping over three thousand people in the middle. Escape was impossible and, when the central arch collapsed into the river, all were either burned, crushed or drowned.

Gary Gilmore was sentenced to die facing a Utah firing squad for double murder in 1977. In an old factory building he was tied to an office chair in front of a mattress, which was positioned there to stop ricochets; he was then blindfolded and a single spotlight was trained on him. The members of the firing squad were concealed behind a screen, which had holes through which they sighted their rifles on the piece of white cloth covering his heart. A single salvo was sufficient.

Sawing a victim in two was practised by the Chinese; the criminal stood upright, secured between two boards, and two men used a two-handed saw to cut him vertically in half, starting at the head.

In Middle Eastern countries the rules governing contemporary execution by stoning to death are clearly defined. The victim, tied hand and foot, is buried in sand up to his neck and a sheet is spread over his head, doubtless to conceal the terrified expression on his face from the crowd of spectators. The size of the stones thrown is critical: if too large, they would kill too quickly; if too small, they wouldn't be classed as stones. Somewhere in between is acceptable.

Footman Norman Ross was executed in January 1751 for cutting his mistress' throat. According to Scottish law, he was sentenced to have the hand which had held the knife severed, then to be hanged. The rope was thrown over the gallows, its end, according to custom, being held by four chimney sweeps, who pulled it and so strangled the victim. The felon's body was afterwards hung in chains.

Sado-masochist and cannibal Albert Howard Fish not only murdered at least fifteen young children but ate some of their flesh; he was quoted as saying that 'it tastes something like veal or chicken; little girls have more flavour than boys.' In January 1936 he was executed in Sing Sing's electric chair; two charges of current were required, since the first was believed to have been ineffective because of the 29 needles he had, over the years, inserted in his genital area to obtain sexual gratification. Society was also gratified by his demise.

Just because a criminal had died didn't mean that justice should not take its course. In August 1888 an Oriental salt-smuggler was killed while being captured; his corpse was carried into the courtroom, found guilty and condemned to be beheaded. And duly was.

Believed to be England's greatest mass murderer at the time, Mary Ann Cotton never hesitated to slay her husbands or her children in order to obtain the insurance money. Regarded as being responsible for poisoning fifteen or possibly as many as 25 victims, she was hanged in March 1873 by executioner William Calcraft, who was not noted for his attention to detail; the length of the rope was too short, and Mary Ann's body kicked and struggled for three minutes before becoming as limp as her many victims.

Mazzatello might sound like an Italian cheese but in fact was what must have been one of the most brutal methods of execution imaginable. Eighteenth- and nineteenth-century Italian criminals condemned to death would have to mount the scaffold, where the black-clad and masked executioner was waiting, leaning on a heavy long-handled mallet. After prayers had been said, the executioner would move round behind the felon, swing the weapon a couple of times to gain momentum, then bring it down as hard as possible on his victim's head. He would then finish the task by slitting the unconscious man's throat.

Because Jeremiah Brandreth, Isaac Ludlum and William Turner were the ringleaders of riots in 1817, they were sentenced to be hanged, drawn and quartered, but this was reduced to being hanged until dead and then beheaded; an axe, based on the one in the Tower of London, was used to decapitate them. A vast crowd had gathered to watch the hangings but, when the axeman got to work, they all ran away.

Flaying alive was not confined to Eastern countries; in 1366 the chamberlain of the French Count de Rouci suffered that slow death for betraying Laon to the English forces, and the Constable of Armagnac, caught by the enemy, came to a similar agonising end.

Mata Hari, a spy in World War I, was sentenced to die before a firing squad. Her execution took place on 15 October 1917 in the moat of a chateau in Vincennes, France. Calm and self-possessed, she declared her innocence and, when her arms were bound to the execution post, refused to be blindfolded; instead she looked calmly at the soldiers drawn up facing her, as they sighted along the barrels of their rifles. Although she was struck by twelve bullets, she was seen to move, and the officer in charge had to administer the *coup de grâce* with a single shot to the head from his pistol. Her body, which had so entranced audiences with its sinuous and erotic movements during her dances, was later taken away and dissected by surgical students.

When King Amanullah of Afghanistan and his brother abdicated in January 1929, Bacha Sachao took over the throne. Ruthless to a degree, his method of dealing with those who questioned his right to power was to have them 'blown from a cannon's mouth' – disembowelled by an artillery shell.

Before the discovery of anaesthetics, surgery was performed with the help of the 'holders down', sturdy hospital porters who were summoned by a bell before an operation to pin the patient down on the operating table while the scalpel-wielders got to work.

William, Lord Russell, was unjustly accused of being a member of an assassination conspiracy known as the Rye House Plot and in 1683 was sentenced to death. He asked how much he should give the executioner and, when told ten guineas (£10 10s.) was customary, said with a smile that it was a pretty thing to have to give a fee to have one's head cut off. The executioner clumsily took two strokes of the axe and, because the weapon was then embedded in the block, had to use his knife to sever the few sinews still joining the head to the body. It was of no consolation to his Lordship that later monarchs, William and Mary, reversed his attainder (decreed that he was innocent of the charge).

In 1951 murderer Elisio Mares was sentenced to be executed in Utah, USA, by a four-man firing squad. Either they didn't know the location of his heart or were just poor marksmen, but after the salvo the doctor discovered that all four bullets had penetrated the right-hand side of Mares' chest, and he had bled to death.

Four centuries ago some criminals in Japan were tortured by being buried upside down, with just the lower part of their body, and one arm, remaining above ground. Only when they indicated, by hand movements, that they were prepared to confess to their crimes were they eventually released – to be tried and executed.

London's Fleet River, long since covered over, was earlier known as Fleet Ditch, and was a foul-smelling open sewer for centuries. In 1763 it was reported that a drunken barber fell into it in the winter darkness and was found the next morning, not drowned but standing upright in the mud, frozen to death.

The three Van Wormer brothers were electrocuted in 1903 and pronounced dead, but one of them was later seen to move. A medical check revealed that he had a larger heart than usual – so he was taken back and electrocuted again.

At least eight people were killed and many injured when explosives, packed not into a car but into panniers on a horse, blew up in a crowded market in Columbia in 2003. Militant rebels were blamed for the slaughter.

In 1842 a young woman committed suicide by jumping from the top of the Monument in London, following which an iron fence was erected round the platform. And three years later a man ended his life by leaping from the Whispering Gallery in St Paul's

Cathedral, after which, it is assumed, the holy place was recon-
secrated.

The USA had the electric chair, England had the rope, France had
the guillotine – and India had the elephant! In the eighteenth century, criminals in that country were held spread-eagled on their
backs on the ground, their heads secured between two iron
plates, and then the elephant would advance from behind. Its
driver, the mahout, would give the necessary orders, upon which
the beast would gently place one foot on the victim's head. Any
further description would be superfluous.

At Exeter in 1789, highwayman William Snow felt the noose
start to tighten round his neck as the cart in which he was standing moved away – then suddenly realised that instead of
swinging, half-strangled, he was still alive, the rope having freed
itself from the gallows arm. Immediately he was seized by the
hangman and his assistant and pushed on to the cart again. Gasps
of horror came from the crowd, but Snow slowly looked around,
then exclaimed, 'Good people, be not hurried; I am not hurried –
I can wait a little!' Nor did he have long to wait – and neither did
the crowd!

Leo Frank may have thought he'd got away with murder when
his death sentence was commuted to one of imprisonment, but
the residents of Georgia, USA, shocked at the enormity of his
crime – he had strangled fourteen-year-old Mary Phagan –
thought otherwise. So they abducted him from jail, took him
nearly two hundred miles to where his victim had been born and
there hanged him.

A harsh and primitive torture existed in Bengal in earlier centuries. In 1614 a visitor described how a woman was secured to
a stake positioned in a deep hole, which was then filled with earth

up to her armpits. She was left there, deprived of food and water, and subjected to the heat of the sun and the attention of insects, for three days; if she survived, she was pardoned.

Hara-kiri, Japanese for 'belly-cutting', means just that. Using a short sword nine inches long with a razor-sharp blade, the victim, naked to the waist, inserts the weapon deep into the left-hand side of his stomach, pulls it across horizontally, then draws it upwards, disembowelling himself.

In earlier days, increasing one's income by counterfeiting coins was severely frowned on by the authorities. In 1786 Phoebe Harris was burned at the stake in front of Newgate Prison before a crowd of 20,000 people. The *Mercury* reported, without the slightest semblance of sympathy, that 'Some scattered remains of the woman were perceptible at half past ten in the morning, and the fire had completely burnt out by twelve o'clock.'

When caught by members of the anti-fascist maquis at the end of World War II, the Italian dictator Benito Mussolini and his mistress Clara Petacci were shot and their cadavers put on display, hanging upside down.

Dead-Easy Recipes

Many concoctions were tried by women intent on poisoning their husbands, but few were as exotic as those employed by American Lena Miller in 1813; her recipe consisted of soaked and powdered laurel leaves, brass filings, laudanum, indigo – and a small green snake boiled in coffee!

A prospective employee's CV doesn't include everything, and so, when the records of Graham Young were checked after the mysterious deaths of two workmen and severe illnesses of other members of the firm, the manager was horrified to discover that not only had Young earlier poisoned his stepmother and tried to kill his father and sister by the same method, but he had also spent nine years incarcerated in Broadmoor, an institution for the criminally insane. Found guilty in 1972, Young died in jail eighteen years later.

When husband A wants to marry wife B, the logical solution is to eliminate husband B and wife A, a plan adopted in 1911 in India by Dr Clark and Mrs Fulham. He provided the arsenic, diagnosed Mr Fulham's symptoms as heat stroke and administered gelsemine, resulting in the demise of obstacle number one. Four assassins were then hired to dispose of Mrs Clark, which they did, using a sword. But when incriminating love letters from Clark were found in Mrs Fulham's bedroom, the game was up. The doctor was hanged in Allahabad but Mrs Fulham, pregnant with his child, was only imprisoned. Ironically she died shortly afterwards – of heat stroke.

Marie Frazier injected her mother and her husband with arsenic, from which they both died, and also attempted to kill her daughter in the same way. Arrested in 1979, she fled, marrying again a year later. Then, telling her new husband she had to visit a relative in Houston, she had obituary notices published in the newspapers announcing her death and the cremation of her body. She then returned to her grieving husband, explaining that she was her dead sister's twin, and joined in the commiserations. Police investigations revealed the truth, and she was found guilty and imprisoned for life. However, in 1987, while out on weekend licence, she failed to return and lived rough until recaptured; taken to hospital, she died shortly afterwards.

Poison can be given to the victim in food or drink, but on the end of an umbrella? Yet that is how poison was administered to Bulgarian political refugee Georgi Markov as he walked across Waterloo Bridge in 1978. He felt something touch the back of his leg, heard a guttural apology, thought no more about it – and was dead within 48 hours. The post mortem revealed that a deadly poison, ricin, had been concealed within a tiny pellet only 1.52mm in diameter, which had two small holes to allow the poison to enter the bloodstream; the pellet had been hidden in the tip of the umbrella used as a deadly weapon by the stranger, who, it was later ascertained, had been a member of the Bulgarian secret police.

It was believed that Johann Hoch, the 'Stockyards Bluebeard', induced as many as 35 childless widows to marry him, then poisoned them for their money using arsenic, supplies of which he concealed in a fountain pen. In February 1906 he was hanged in Chicago.

Feeling disappointed at failing promotion is one thing; murdering your more successful colleagues is another. When fellow officers in the Austrian army in 1912 received nerve tonic pills and one of them died, suspicion fell on Lieutenant Adolph Hofrichter, who had failed promotion to the rank of captain. His protests of innocence were rejected when young women came forward to claim that he had drugged and sexually assaulted them, and the court replaced his officer's uniform with that of a convict, which he wore for the next twenty years.

A method of execution adopted by the Greeks involved hemlock, an umbelliferous Eurasian plant which is highly toxic. The criminal would be required to drink a solution of it and, after it had permeated his system, would be allowed to lie down while the deadly effects slowly overcame him.

Sadamichi Hirasawa chose an ingenious but bizarre way to rob a Tokyo bank in 1948: posing as a public health official, he persuaded the sixteen employees present to drink what he described as the antidote to a local outbreak of dysentery. Far from being beneficial, the dosage consisted of potassium cyanide, and, as the staff writhed in agony on the floor, he calmly emptied the tills and departed, leaving twelve of his victims in their death throes. Hirasawa was later arrested but doubts about his guilt persisted and, although sentenced to death, he spent over thirty years in prison.

Margaret Davey was boiled alive in a cauldron at Smithfield, London, in 1542, for poisoning the family for whom she worked.

Michael Barber discovered his wife had a lover so he beat her up; she retaliated by serving up a steak-and-kidney pie for dinner next day, to which she'd added just a soupçon of a herbicide called Paraquat as flavouring. He died in agony; she collected his insurance and rejoined the boyfriend. And in 1982 she received a life sentence.

Because a cook named Richard Roose killed at least seventeen people in 1531 by poisoning their porridge, a special Act of Parliament was passed condemning him to be boiled to death. And so he was.

In a book published in 1750 it was claimed that an illness could be cured if the dried body of a dead toad was placed in a silk bag and worn about the invalid's neck, 'although two legs from a live toad were better, for as it [the toad] pined, wasted and died, the distemper would likewise waste and die.'

For opposing the marriage of the Earl of Somerset and Lady Essex, the couple had Sir Thomas Overbury committed to the Tower of London, where he was poisoned by a Mrs Turner, who, over many weeks, arranged for his meals to include powdered diamonds, lapis cortilus, white arsenic, mercury, 'great spiders', aquafortis and cantharides. Hardly surprisingly, he eventually died. Mrs Turner was hanged, wearing the yellow ruff and cuffs she had introduced into the royal court; similar accessories were also worn for the occasion by the hangman. Yellow starch rapidly went out of fashion.

A magazine published in 1936 included a recipe submitted by an Oxfordshire woman to cure whooping cough. The main ingredient was a mouse, which first had to be skinned, of course, then all its bones removed; after that, she said, all one has to do is fry it and feed it to the sick child.

In order to prove that Dr Robert Buchanan killed his wife, prosecuting counsel had to kill a cat! It was suspected that the doctor used morphine, a poison which can be identified by the pinpoints it causes to appear in the victim's eyes; there were none in his wife's but it was claimed that he could have prevented such incriminating signs by dropping belladonna (deadly nightshade) into her eyes. To prove that, the prosecutor produced a cat in the courtroom and proceeded first to kill it with morphine, then to apply the belladonna to its sightless eyes. Nothing further could be said in the doctor's defence and in July 1895 he died in the electric chair. Regrettably, no one was charged with the murder of the innocent feline.

In the 1930s an Austrian woman, Martha Lowenstein, and her partner Emil chose an unusual method of making money. He took out an insurance policy for £10,000 against injury, and a week later was rushed to hospital with a severed leg, claiming that it had happened when he was cutting down a tree and the axe slipped. But he didn't have a leg to stand on – or at least he only had one – when the surgeons discovered that three blows had been struck! Martha had wielded the axe, and both received prison sentences for attempting to defraud the insurance company. Emil died later and, when two other people passed away under suspicious circumstances, Martha was arrested. Poison was found in all three bodies, and she was beheaded in December 1938.

It was claimed in a medical book written in 1659 that the way to cure a man of drinking too much was to add a live eel to his ale without him being aware of it. His reactions on draining the tankard no doubt proved highly effective!

There was not much future in being a husband in small villages in the remote province of Szolnok, Hungary, in the 1920s. For fifteen years many wives decided they'd be better off as widows or free to wed younger men, and, in three of the villages alone, the death toll amounted to 98, some wives shedding as many as two or three husbands as the years went by. In one area of the province poison was supplied by two 'wise women', Madam Zazekof and Madam Papai, who, as well as having the medical knowhow to cure dandruff and corns, provided toxic ingredients such as arsenic (obtained by soaking it off fly-papers) or rat poison with which to flavour hubby's meals, or substituted toadstools for mushrooms in soup. These recipes didn't come cheap, of course: the charges levied against their female customers ranged from a load of hay to the equivalent of £6–8. In other villages the prescriptions were supplied by two midwives, who, when the police got on their track, hanged themselves in a barn. At least fifty women were finally charged with their husbands' murders; some were executed, the others sentenced to long terms of imprisonment.

What food was best to eat was just as important nine hundred years ago as it is now. The medical school at Salerno, Italy, prescribed the following: 'Water drinking at meals chills the stomach, wine is preferable, but if very thirsty, drink from a cool fountain, rainwater is best; onions rubbed on the scalp restores fallen hair, honey mixed with chervil cures cancer; figs breed lice and stir up lust; pork is inferior to lamb unless taken with much wine; eating eels hurts the voice; cheese eaten with eels requires much drink; sage soothes the nerves and quiets trembling hands; and pepper, white or black, aids digestion, cures coughs and checks fever.'

Belladonna, Italian for 'beautiful woman', also known as deadly nightshade, is a plant from which poison is extracted. In earlier centuries women would use it as eyedrops, thereby enlarging their pupils to make themselves more alluring. Dodgy even in the eyes, in the mouth it's fatal.

In 1848 it was decided by the owners of Liverpool Zoological Gardens that an elephant which had killed its keeper would have to be put down. Two ounces of prussic acid and 25 grains of aconite, a deadly poison, were given to the elephant in a bun, but this toxic dose only made the animal slightly uneasy for a few minutes. Accordingly a detachment of the Third Rifles, consisting of fifteen soldiers, was sent for; after the first volley of shots, the elephant staggered and leaned against the wall of the enclosure; a second volley followed, killing the beast instantly.

It was reported in 1929 that residents of the Blue Ridge Mountains of Virginia believed that the remedy for tuberculosis, pleurisy and similar ailments was to swallow one live snail before going to bed, every day for nine days. The snail would survive by eating what it could in the patient's stomach, but before it died its slimy trail would circulate throughout the body and alleviate the irritation present in the lungs.

Cooking programmes seem to proliferate on television channels nowadays but one recipe has so far been neglected. In 1754 it was reported that a young man, meeting a female celebrity of the day, pulled her shoe off, filled it with champagne and drank her health. To carry the compliment further, he ordered it to be made ready to eat for supper, whereupon the cook pulled the damask upper part into fine shreds and tossed it up into ragout; he minced the sole; and he cut the wooden heel into very fine slices, fried them in butter and placed them round the dish for garnish. It was stated that 'the company testified their affection for the lady by eating very heartily of this exquisite impromptu'. Now there's a culinary challenge!

ROYAL DEEDS AND MISDEEDS

Juana, a sixteenth-century Spanish queen, was known as 'Crazy Jane' because she refused to have her royal husband's corpse buried, but kept it with her on her travels.

After Anne Boleyn was beheaded on the orders of her husband Henry VIII, her eyes and lips were seen to move. Some medical authorities subsequently believed that consciousness can continue for an unknown length of time after decapitation because blood remains present in the brain. After all, organs removed for transplant purposes remain 'alive' for some time, and as the brain is an organ . . .

In 1848 Prince Louis Napoleon, later Emperor of France, lived in London, and when widespread riots were instigated by members of the Chartists, a volatile political party, the Prince was sworn in as a Special Constable of the Metropolitan Police.

The Duke of Oxford, while asking formal permission to withdraw from his audience with Queen Elizabeth I, had the misfortune to break wind. Abashed, he went abroad, and, on his return seven years later, the Queen welcomed him back graciously, saying, 'My Lord, I had forgot the fart!'

During the seventeenth-century war between Spain and the Low Countries, Ostend was besieged by the Spaniards for such a long time that the Spanish Archduchess vowed she would not change her linen (underwear) until the town was taken. Three years passed before it surrendered, and the resultant dingy hue of the lady's undies was promptly christened *l'Isabeau*, or the 'Isabella' colour.

When Queen Caroline, consort of George II, died in 1737, her grief-stricken husband missed her so much that he had all the queens removed from the Palace's packs of playing cards.

Elizabeth I's corpse 'suddenly burst asunder with such a crack that it splitted the wood, lead and serecloth' because it hadn't been embalmed.

The architectural layout and ornamentation of the Escurial, Madrid's royal palace, was designed in the form of a gridiron by order of Philip II, whose patron saint St Lawrence had been burned to death while secured to one.

After Queen Catherine de Valois died in 1437, her corpse was not given a Christian burial but was left displayed to the public in Westminster Abbey, exposed from the waist upwards, until it was finally interred 339 years later, in 1776.

King John was buried between the bodies of two Saxon monks and wearing a monk's habit, hoping thereby to fool the Lord on Judgment Day.

Arabella Stuart, James I's cousin, died insane in the Tower of London in September 1615. Her corpse, so frail and wasted that her skull and bones could almost be seen through her parchment-like skin, was taken by boat along the Thames and, in a coffin without any name plate on it, interred in the royal vaults of Westminster Abbey.

The corpse of William II was transported to Winchester, for burial, in a dung-cart.

Oliver Cromwell reputedly held up the head of his arch-enemy Charles I to make sure it had been severed.

George II died of a heart attack while on the lavatory.

When Queen Anne died, sarcastic courtiers suggested that because of her obesity she would need a square coffin.

The dysentery which caused the death of King John in 1216 was brought about by a meal of peaches, wine and fresh cider.

Queen Anne gave birth to eighteen children, yet none of them lived to reach maturity; nor did the ten children – five sons and five daughters – of James II.

After his execution Charles I's head was sewn back on to his torso so that a portrait of him could be painted.

Katherine Howard, wife of Henry VIII, sentenced to die beneath the axe, rehearsed kneeling over the block on the evening before her execution.

Anne of Austria, mother of Louis XIV, stipulated that her heart be removed through an aperture in her side and buried separately.

The Holy Roman Emperor Charlemagne was buried at Aachen, Germany, seated upright in a chair.

One of Charles I's vertebrae was removed from his entombed body by his doctor and used as a salt cellar. It was later returned to Queen Victoria who, not amused, ordered that it be reverently returned to the dead king's coffin.

William III was killed when his horse stumbled over a mole-hill and threw him.

James I was violently opposed to smoking. Whether the two thieves who broke into his tomb were aware of this is not known – but they left a broken clay pipe behind them!

Anne Boleyn's decapitated corpse was buried in an old arrow-chest, no coffin having been obtained in advance.

Doctors beware! Two surgeons who failed to cure the wife of Gutram, King of Burgundy, of the plague in AD 580, were executed on her tomb; in 1337 a surgeon was thrown into the River Oder for failing to cure John of Bohemia of blindness; and after Pope John XII died, his friends had the surgeon flayed to death.

Boadicea, the first-century Queen of the Iceni, captured London from the Romans but, when her forces were defeated, was caught and poisoned herself. Her corpse was buried in the capital, allegedly in ground now covered by platform 10 of Liverpool Street railway station.

The head of James IV of Scotland, slain at Flodden Field in 1518, is buried in Wood Green Church cemetery, London.

The carving on the tomb of Henry VIII's fourth wife, Anne of Cleves, who died in 1557, includes what is believed to be the first example of the skull and cross bones decoration in England.

When Queen Christina of Holstein's coffin was opened, centuries after her death, her royal robes and regalia, were present; so was everything but her head!

73

Following the execution by guillotine of Louis XVI during the French Revolution, the buttons from his coat, pieces of his shirt and locks of his hair were offered for sale as souvenirs.

A skeleton believed at the time to be that of Queen Boadicea was discovered bricked up in a wall of Rhuddlan parish church in North Wales in the 1930s, together with pots inscribed with the letter 'B'.

King Harold was killed on receiving an arrow in his eye at the Battle of Hastings in 1066.

Although Queen Mary, 'Bloody Mary', reigned for only six years, nearly three hundred Protestants – archbishops, bishops and commoners – were committed to the flames. In one day, at Stratford-le-Bow, thirteen people were burned alive, two of them women.

Ananda Mahidol, King of Siam, was found dead in his palace in June 1946. He was believed by his devout subjects to be the 'Divine Lord of Life' and, among other restrictions, his subjects were forbidden to touch his holy person. This prohibition made it more than a little difficult for the medical personnel charged with investigating his death to carry out the post mortem, but it was not the first time such awkward situations had arisen in that country: eleven of the previous 33 monarchs had either been murdered or had their rivals done away with. Eventually all obstacles were overruled, murder was proved and those responsible were duly executed.

The remains of Margaret Pole, Countess of Salisbury, beheaded on the orders of Henry VIII, lie interred in the Chapel Royal of St Peter ad Vincula within the Tower of London; reportedly one of her thigh-bones was once shown to the King of Siam!

'Touching for the King's Evil' was highly popular in early centuries, since it was believed that royal contact had the power to cure many diseases. It reached its peak in the time of Charles II, who reportedly 'touched' nearly 24,000 of his subjects during the first four years of his reign.

When Emperor Charles V announced his intention to visit the French town of Douai, the residents prepared a grand reception, with flowers, bands and triumphal arches. But at the last minute they realised that the gibbet situated near the town's gates was occupied by the cadaver of a hanged felon – so they took him down, put a clean white shirt on him and hanged him up again.

A marble urn in Westminster Abbey, designed by Sir Christopher Wren, is believed to contain the remains of the 'Two Little Princes' murdered in the Tower of London.

Guildford Dudley, Lady Jane Grey's husband, was beheaded on Tower Hill. She saw his decapitated body being carried back on a hurdle, en route to the Royal Chapel, as she was being escorted to Tower Green to be executed by the axe.

Many royal coffins in Westminster Abbey have small lead boxes attached to them containing the occupant's heart and other internal organs.

At her death, the body of Anne of Denmark, consort of James I and a tall lady, required a coffin at least 6ft 7ins in length.

When the coffin of Philip II of Spain was opened, it was found to contain one body but two skulls.

Prince Imperial Eugene Louis Jean Joseph, son of Emperor Napoleon III, was stabbed to death while fighting the Zulus in 1879.

The fee received by executioner Richard Brandon for decapitating Charles I was £30, an orange stuck full of cloves and a handkerchief from the King's pocket.

An attempted assassination of George III occurred on 2 August 1786; as he was leaving St James' Palace, a woman stepped forward and, under the pretext of handing him a petition, stabbed him with a knife. Fortunately the courteous act of bowing to the lady saved the King's life, for the blow was deflected by the royal waistcoat.

A foreign visitor to London described Elizabeth I, then 65, as 'very majestic; her face oblong, fair but wrinkled; her eyes small, yet black and pleasant; her Nose a little crooked; her lips narrow and her Teeth black, a defect the English seem subject to, from their great use of sugar. She wore false, red hair, her hands were small, her Fingers long; her Breast was uncovered, as all English ladies have it till they marry.' At that time, however, 'her maids had gotten false looking-glasses, that the Queen might not see her own wrinkles and her goggle-throat [a pendant gullet].'

Ever fearful of being assassinated, James I always wore stiletto-proof quilted doublets in public.

Louis IX of France decreed that blasphemers should be punished by having their brow branded, lips burned and tongue skewered with a hot iron.

James II of Scotland met his death in 1437, being killed on the battlefield when a nearby cannon exploded on firing.

After the Battle of Bosworth in 1485 the corpse of the vanquished Richard III was, as reported by historian Richard Grafton, 'taken to Leicester, naked and despoiled to the skin and nothing left about him, not as much as a clout [cloth] to cover his privy members, and was trussed behind a man at arms called Blaunche Senglier, or White Boar, like a hog or a calf, the head and arms hanging on the one side of the horse, and the legs on the other, all besprinkled with mire and blood.'

When King John's tomb was opened in 1797 someone stole a finger bone as a souvenir; a piece of flesh was also taken and used as fishing bait.

In a vain attempt to save the life of the dying Charles II, court doctors administered blood-letting; an emetic of orange infusion in white wine and white vitriol in peony water; hiera picra; white hellibore roots; powdered cowslip flowers; sal ammoniac in milk water; spirit of human skull; Peruvian bark, and pearl julep. His head was shaved and blisters applied, and cephalic plasters combined with spurge and Burgundy pitch in equal parts (including pigeon's dung) were applied to the soles of his feet. All to no avail, for he then died of chronic Bright's disease.

After the deaths of George II and his consort Caroline, their coffins were placed next to each other, the adjoining sides being removed so that their remains could mingle.

While awaiting burial Henry VIII's leaden coffin sprang a leak, and the blood which dripped on to the chapel pavement was licked up by dogs.

Frederick Louis, son of George II, died after being struck by a tennis ball, the blow resulting in a burst abscess.

After Edward IV died in 1483, to dispel the rumour that he had been assassinated, his embalmed corpse, naked to the waist, was displayed in the Royal Chapel of Westminster Palace for three days, during which a never-ending queue of members of the public filed slowly past to view their late monarch.

After the Battle of Corrichie in 1562, the Earl of Huntley, one of those defeated by the forces of Mary, Queen of Scots, died of a heart attack, but was not allowed to escape the due course of justice just because of that; his coffin, containing his embalmed cadaver, was stood upright, its lid removed, facing the members of the Privy Council, who then proceeded solemnly to find 'him' guilty of treason.

King John was more mentally unstable than downright cruel. It was reported that on one occasion he groaned, 'Why did my mother bear me to misery and shame?', then gnashed his teeth and started to gnaw sticks before throwing them away half-chewed.

Queen Eleanor, consort of Henry II, was by tradition entitled to all the dues paid for corn and wool cargoes offloaded at one London dock, Queenhithe, but this proved so unpopular with the citizens that when, en route from the Tower to Windsor, she passed under London Bridge, they showed their displeasure by pelting her with rotten eggs and chicken bones and shouting 'Drown the witch!'

The assumption that all medieval men were small is not altogether correct. When the coffin of Edward IV, buried in 1483, was opened in 1789, his skeleton was found to measure 6ft. 3ins.

James I's tongue was excessively large 'which made him speak full in the mouth, to drink very uncomely, as if eating his drink, which came out into the cup from each side of his mouth; he never washed his hands, but rubbed his finger tips slightly with the wet end of a napkin, and would never change his clothes until worn out to very rags.'

When the tomb of the Holy Roman Emperor Charles the Great (AD 742–814) was opened it was found that his fingernails had grown through the gloves that he wore; one of his teeth was stolen as a souvenir.

In the reign of Henry I (1100–1135) the coffin of Edward the Confessor (died 1066) was opened in the royal presence; it was reported that the body was lying as if only asleep, the joints supple, the flesh firm and white and the face, framed by white hair and a long beard, as rosy and fresh as in life. Gundulf, Bishop of Rochester, who was present, attempted to pull a hair from the holy beard to keep as a relic, but failed.

Despite Edward I ordering that after his death his flesh should be boiled away and his bones carried in the vanguard of his army, his remains were buried in Westminster Abbey.

The first member of a British royal family to be legally cremated was Princess Louise, daughter of Queen Victoria, in 1943.

When Lady Buchan supported the claim of Robert the Bruce to be King of Scotland, Edward I wreaked revenge by confining her in a cage suspended from an outside wall of Berwick Castle for four years.

On his deathbed Henry VIII summoned his archbishop Cranmer to his side and, opening one of his small steel-grey eyes, muttered, 'All is lost!' then sank back, a corpse.

For many centuries effigies of sovereigns were made and displayed on or near their coffins. That of James I resembled a gigantic wooden doll with jointed arms and legs, its face painted, its wig, beard and eyebrows made of hair and stuck on.

Following her execution in 1587, Mary, Queen of Scots, was buried not in London or Edinburgh but in Peterborough Cathedral. Only years later was her body brought to London and entombed in Westminster Abbey.

Queen Mary died on 17 November 1558 and her embalmed corpse lay in state in St James' Palace. Unusually, the body was clad in the dress of a nun rather than a queen; only her effigy wore royal robes.

When the scourge of smallpox swept through Europe in the 1600s, not even royalty could escape its ravages. Charles IX of France was so severely scarred that he appeared to have two noses; Louis XIV contracted it, as did Louis XV, to whom it proved fatal. In England Queen Mary II became a victim in 1694, and in the following century sixty million people across the Continent died of the disease.

Queen Anne, consort of James I, died on 2 March 1619 but her body had to lie in state in Somerset House until May while the funeral costs were discussed, since the royal purse was empty at the time.

After the death of Edward the Confessor, miraculous cures were said to be obtained merely by touching the coffin, and sick people were allowed to crouch and pray in the niches within the shrine.

When Queen Isabella, widow of Edward II, died, she was buried with her husband's heart in a silver box resting on her bosom.

Following the birth of Prince Edward by Jane Seymour, members of the court flocked into the bedroom to celebrate the great event, but the frenzy in the crowded room proved so taxing for Her Majesty, as she lay propped up in bed, that she had a relapse and died shortly afterwards.

The saying 'You can't take it with you' may be true, but when the Eastern ruler Ali Pasha lay dying he didn't want to leave it behind – even though the 'it' was not only his wife Vasilika but the fabulous Piggott diamond, which weighed 49 carats and, even then, in the late eighteenth century, was valued at £40,000. He changed his mind, but only so far as his spouse was concerned, and he ordered his aide-de-camp, Captain D'Anglas, to crush the diamond to powder while he watched. So the officer obediently put the gem in a bowl and with a club-shaped pestle reduced it to dust – something he regretted for the rest of his life.

Henry VI was considered a martyr by many: so much so that, after his murder in the Tower of London in 1471, those suffering illnesses would don a hat placed on his tomb and then wear it, in the hope of a speedy cure for their ailments.

As a child Charles, son of James I, was slow in learning to speak and incapable of standing upright unsupported. His father therefore suggested that the string of his tongue be cut and that he be put in iron boots to strengthen his sinews, but luckily he was overruled by his advisors.

Emma, mother of Edward the Confessor (1044-1066), was accused of being too friendly with the Bishop of Winchester and, in order to make her confess, was put to the Ordeal: made to walk barefoot and blindfolded over nine glowing hot irons. This she did and, on having her eyes uncovered, knelt and gave thanks at having passed over them unscathed, thereby proving her innocence.

Edward VII had an eye for the ladies, as was revealed when, during army manoeuvres on Salisbury Plain, he was caught taking part in less martial exercises in his tent with an actress.

After the marriage of James I's favourite Sir Philip Herbert to Lady Susan Vere, which took place at Whitehall in December 1604, His Majesty took an active role on the following morning: clad in shirt and nightgown, he greeted the newly-weds before they had risen and then spent some time upon and in the bed with them.

George III, prone to fits of insanity, once reportedly talked at length to an oak tree, assuming it to be the King of Prussia.

When, during the Crimean War, gossip ran rife that Queen Victoria's German husband Prince Albert was influencing Her Majesty's decisions in favour of the enemy, and that both had been arrested and taken to the Tower of London, thousands sought admittance, hoping to witness the royal prisoners.

During the reign of Edward I in the 1300s, the jewels and other royal valuables were stored in the Treasury of the Palace of Westminster. When some were reported missing, His Majesty was outraged. The finger of suspicion pointed to the clergy and monks who lived in the nearby Abbey, and their guilt was substantiated after investigations had been carried out by the Lord Mayor and the Master of the King's Wardrobe. Severe penalties were immediately inflicted: the sub-prior of the Abbey was put to death, the abbot and 48 monks were arrested and imprisoned in the Tower of London, and strict measures were taken against others. The exact punishments were not recorded, but five hundred years later Sir Gilbert Scott, Dean of Westminster Abbey, discovered what were identified as pieces of human skin stretched and nailed across the Treasury door.

Edward I's dying wish was that every two years his tomb should be opened and his cerecloth (shroud) renewed. After his burial in 1307 this gruesome procedure of disturbing his slowly moulding remains continued for 92 years, finally ceasing with the death of Richard II in 1399.

There was confusion at the altar during the coronation of Henry II, when the Bishop of Salisbury – rather than the Archbishop of Canterbury, whose role it usually was – went to place the crown on the King's head. The change in the programme was necessary because the Archbishop suffered from incurable palsy, and a shaking hand bearing the crown could have missed the target altogether. Unfortunately no one had told the Archbishop of the change; he attempted to seize the crown and stumbled and, had not the Bishop of Salisbury made a rapid save, the crown would have fallen to the ground. Salisbury completed the essential act and Henry II became King.

Henry VIII was so determined that the Tudor line should continue to rule that he arranged for his son Edward to be crowned before he himself had died.

When James I died in 1635 his corpse was placed in a lead coffin which was then encased in a larger wooden coffin-shaped container, consisting of two logs of solid timber hollowed out to the required dimensions.

Few graves in cemeteries lack gravestones inscribed with the names of those buried beneath, yet oddly enough it was discovered in 1869 that, since the days of Elizabeth I, the vaults in Westminster Abbey in which royalty had been entombed had been left without any name or mark to indicate their position within the building.

A highly significant part of the coronation ceremony is the anointing of the body of the sovereign with consecrated oil. When, in 1483, the Duke of Gloucester and his wife Anne of Warwick were being crowned, attendants ceremonially stripped them both to the waist to receive the anointing, the dukes gathering round the new King, the bishops and ladies around the Queen.

After George IV had died in 1830, his mistress Lady Conyingham and her relatives proceeded to ransack his apartments in Windsor Castle, hastily stowing valuable pictures, clocks and silverware in their waiting carriages. When the household staff arrived to prepare the place for the next occupant, they discovered a treasure trove of royal memorabilia: letters and locks of hair, some still with powder adhering to the strands, from female admirers, and ladies' gloves that had been given to His Majesty at balls, the opera or the races. Cash to the value of £10,000 was found hidden, together with scores of pocket books, each containing a small amount of money, ready for possible use. All these items were handed in to the Lord Chamberlain's department, but the remainder of the King's wardrobe – garments, hats, uniforms, boots, whips and canes – was shared out among the staff as souvenirs of their late master (or as nice little earners when sold to collectors or antique dealers).

Not content with having six wives, two of whom he had had executed, Henry VIII anticipated having even more: his will provided for children he might have 'by any other wife after Catherine Parr', his last one.

The death sentence pronounced on Charles I was: 'Whereas for all which treasons and crimes this Court doth adjudge, that the said Charles Stuart, as a tyrant, traitor, murderer, and a public enemy, shall be put to death by the severing of his head from his body.' And so he was, on 30 January 1649.

Four English monarchs were left-handed, James I, George II, George IV and George VI; which, if not exactly macabre, is certainly sinister!

When one of the tombs in Westminster Abbey was entered in the 1870s, a ghastly sight was revealed. In the gloom, a vast pile of leaden coffins could be seen, heaped one upon another in wild confusion, and urns containing the viscera of the corpses were scattered about the floor. One grotesque coffin in the shape of a body held the remains of Henry, Prince of Wales, interred in 1612, while compressed and distorted by the weight of four or five coffins lying on top of them were those of Mary, Queen of Scots, and Arabella Stuart, the skull and bones of the latter clearly visible.

William the Conqueror's consort, Queen Matilda, was only 4ft 2ins tall.

Edward VI, son of Henry VIII and last of the Tudor kings, died young and was buried in Westminster Abbey. His coffin, discovered in 1868, was of lead and very corroded, as was the coffin plate bearing the occupant's name. When the coffin was opened, the King's head was visible; the shroud had rotted away and, although hair normally survives for many centuries, it was apparent that the skull was completely bald, corroborating the historian Froude's description of the King's last and fatal illness, that 'eruptions came out all over his skin, and his hair fell out.'

Edward the Confessor, King of England, son of Ethelred the Unready, was an albino.

Henry VIII, Edward VI, James II, William IV, Mary I, Mary II and Anne all contracted sexual diseases.

Louis XIV, 'Father of the French People', ordained that anyone who uttered eight blasphemies should have his tongue torn out.

It was said that James I 'hunted everything that ran, and knighted everything that crawled', the former being deer and other animals, the latter his favourites, of which he had many.

Taking no chances over his favourable reception on Resurrection Day, Henry VII ordered that after his death ten thousand Masses should be said for his soul.

We take it for granted that coffins are rectangular, with straight sides and squared-off corners, but such receptacles were very different in the seventeenth century, particularly for royalty. The coffin of Henry Frederick, Prince of Wales, who died in 1612, was of lead and human-shaped, with facial features moulded on the head, and the arms and legs even possessing fingers and toes.

Alice Perrers, mistress of Edward III, shed crocodile tears over him as he lay dying, then pulled all the rings from his fingers and kept them.

Henry I did more than attend to the affairs of State; attending to other affairs, he sired 21 illegitimate children.

After Jacques d'Armagnac, Count of Nemours, had been executed on the orders of Louis XI of France, further revenge was exacted on the Count's family: his children were taken to the Bastille prison and their teeth extracted.

Even the highest in the land realised that students could only learn surgery by anatomising human bodies and so, in 1832, the

Duke of Sussex, the youngest son of George III, and the uncle of Queen Victoria gave directions that after death their corpses should be given to surgeons for dissection.

King Basil II (958–1025) conquered the Bulgars, then ordered that the fifteen thousand prisoners of war his army had captured should be blinded.

Elizabeth I is always portrayed as having a creamy complexion; hardly surprising, for her make-up was a mixture of egg, powdered eggshell, borax, alum and poppy seeds.

When mourners called to pay their last respects to the late son of Louis XVI of France as he lay in state in the palace, the Groom of the Chamber would announce the name of the mourner to the corpse in stentorian tones, as if they were attending some state ceremony.

During the marriage celebrations of Louis XVI and Marie Antoinette in 1770, huge crowds flocked to the rue Royale, but disaster struck when thieves stretched ropes across the street, and in the darkness hundreds of people tripped and were trampled on. Children were passed over the heads of the surging crowd, only to be dropped and trodden underfoot. Horses and carriages fell, bodies piled up on each other and some men even tried to hack their way out with their swords; 2,470 people lost their lives in the mad scramble to escape.

Queen Charlotte, consort of George III, gave birth to fifteen children before she reached the age of 38.

Oliver Cromwell was a first cousin eleven times removed of the late Princess Diana.

Benarbo Visconti, a fourteenth century ruler of Lombardy, loathed the Church's preachings so much that on one occasion he publicly burned four nuns and a friar at the stake.

When George IV was being crowned, his estranged consort Queen Caroline pleaded to be allowed into the Abbey and crowned with him, but was forcibly prevented by the ushers at the doors.

In order to ensure that a child born to a queen is genuinely hers and not an impostor smuggled into the bedroom, the Secretary of State of the day had to bear witness to the baby's royal authenticity. This tradition was not discontinued until the 1930s.

The last queen to die in the Tower of London was Elizabeth of York, consort of Henry VII. In February 1503 her body rested there for three days in the Chapel Royal of St John the Evangelist, surrounded by five hundred wax tapers, after which it was embalmed, placed in a coffin and taken in procession to Westminster Abbey, the route brightly illuminated by five thousand torches.

During the coronation of Queen Charlotte in 1760 a highly embarrassing event occurred, as described by the Earl of Orford in a letter to a friend. He wrote: 'Of all the incidents of the day, the most diverting was what happened to the Queen. She had a retiring room, with ALL conveniences, prepared behind the altar. She went there – and in the most INCONVENIENT, what did she find – but the Duke of Newcastle!' Who said unisex loos were a new invention?

During the reign of Henry VIII, the chief of the King's barbers had the duty of reporting to the palace every Saturday night –

that being the royal bath night – and 'if it please the King, to cleanse his head, legs and feet'.

Accidents will happen, even during events of national importance. At his coronation in AD 500, Gunbald, King of Burgundy, was being carried on a sacred shield when he overbalanced and nearly fell off; had he done so he would have been trampled underfoot by the vast crowd of supporters.

Anne Boleyn was beheaded at 9 a.m. on 19 May 1536 and, on each anniversary of that date, for decades past, roses from an anonymous donor are delivered to the Tower of London. There a yeoman warder places them on the inscribed stone covering her remains, in front of the altar in the Chapel Royal of St Peter ad Vincula within the Tower. They are removed only when the blooms have withered.

Panic broke out in London when, in 1745, word came of the Jacobite rebellion and the advance of a Scottish army towards the city. George II packed his bags in readiness to flee to Hanover, but Lady Stafford, one of London's most sought-after hostesses, wrote letters inviting the wives of the Scottish leaders to a soirée.

An anatomical investigation was carried out in 1933 by Professor Wright and Mr Lawrence Tanner of the remains of two boys, believed to be the 'Two Little Princes', discovered in the Tower of London in 1674. They found evidence that the boys were related to each other, that they had been suffocated, that one was aged between twelve and thirteen, the other between nine and eleven. As their approximate birth dates were known, it was concluded that they been murdered before or during the reign of Richard III, not by his successor Henry VII as is sometimes mistakenly assumed.

When war clouds gathered in 1939 George VI offered to intercede with Adolf Hitler 'as one ex-serviceman to another', an offer quickly rejected by the Prime Minister.

The son of Edward III was known as the Black Prince, but he was not aware of the title because it was not given to him until after his death, his 'shroud' being a suit of black armour.

When Charles the Righteous of France was assassinated by Bertholde in 1127, Louis the Bulky sentenced the murderer to death by crucifixion.

Sometimes it just doesn't pay to cheer too loudly on State occasions. On Christmas Day 1066, William the Conqueror was being crowned in Westminster Abbey and, because he'd recently invaded the country, hundreds of his Norman soldiers were on guard outside. At the high point in the ceremony, all the invited guests within acclaimed their new king, but on hearing the noise the soldiers assumed that the congregation were attacking him. Fighting broke out between them and the hundreds of spectators waiting outside for the triumphal procession; many were killed and houses were set on fire, and it was only when William, clad in his coronation robes, appeared at the church door to reassure his troops that what might have been a massacre was quelled.

Edward VII narrowly escaped being shot when visiting Brussels in 1900. He kept the assassin's bullet as a lucky charm.

During World War II, Queen Elizabeth, the Queen Mother, was taught to fire a revolver, in case of invasion.

It's all very well to have a party and invite people, but not when they proceed to wreck the place! Yet that is precisely what happened in June 1881 when the Prince of Wales attended a ball at

Carlton House, London, to which everyone who was anyone had been invited, dukes and duchesses, lords and ladies, dignitaries and service officers. Tables were laden with food and drink, four orchestras played and sixty servants ran backwards and forwards replenishing the guests with wine and delicacies. After the revelries had gone on for several days, the Prince generously decided to invite some of the thirty thousand spectators massed outside watching the merry-making, and within seconds a horde of people poured into the building. The scene quickly became one of devastation: shoeless and gownless women, many in tears, searched desperately for somewhere to hide, while their escorts fought their way out to obtain fresh clothing; tables were overthrown, crockery smashed, silverware stolen, flowers and plants trodden underfoot; outside in the street the Horse Guards struggled to control the mêlée, their rearing mounts causing numerous casualties. Many hours passed before order was restored.

While on the scaffold, Lady Jane Grey handed a prayer-book to an officer, to be given to the Lieutenant of the Tower of London. On a blank page she had inscribed her last emotional and touching words: 'For as muchte as you have desyred so simple a woman to wrighte in so worthye a book, good mayster Lieutenante, therefore I shall as a frende desyre you, and as a christian require you, to call upon God to encline your harte to his lawes, to quicken you in his wayes and not to take the worde of trewethe utterlye oute of your mouthe. Lyve still to dye, that by deathe you may purchas eternall life, and remember howe the ende of Methusael, whoe as we reade in the scriptures was the longest liver that was a manne, died at the laste; foras the precher sayethe, there is a tyme to be borne and a tyme to die; and the daye of deathe is better than the daye of oure birthe. Youres, as ever the Lord knoweth, as a frende, Jane Duddeley.' Then she knelt over the block and the axe descended.

When Charles II regained the throne in 1660, all the Cromwellians who had condemned his father Charles I to be executed by the axe were rounded up and they too were executed. Samuel Pepys, never one to miss any public entertainment, wrote in his diary against 13 October 1660: 'I went out to Charing Cross to see Major-General Harrison hanged, drawn and quartered; which was done there, he looking as cheerful as any man could be in that condition. He was presently cut down [and cut up!], and his head and heart shown to the people, at which there were great shouts of joy.'

While inspecting the Guards in 1935 George V survived an attack by a mentally ill Irishman, who, instead of firing his revolver, threw it at the King, fortunately without causing any injury.

William the Conqueror died when his horse jumped a ditch and he was thrown forward on to the high pommel of his saddle and ruptured his bowel.

A letter to Sir Martin Stuteville dated 16 May 1623 stated that 'there be jewels gone from the Tower to Spain of six hundred thousand pounds value'. It happened that Prince Charles had recently visited that country with the intention of courting the King's daughter: a pure coincidence, of course.

With the exception of Louis XVIII, not one of the monarchs of France ended his life peacefully at the Tuileries for a century: Louis XVI was guillotined in 1793, while Napoleon I died in exile in 1821, as did Napoleon II in 1832, Charles X in 1836 and Napoleon III in 1873.

So great was the crowd at the coronation of Edward II in 1307 that Sir John Bakewell was pushed to the ground and trampled to death.

On the death of the King of Siam in past centuries, mercury was poured into the corpse's mouth, a golden mask placed on the face, and the body seated on a pierced throne, beneath which was a golden vase. After the mercury had cleansed the body, the contents of the vase were ceremonially emptied in the river. The corpse was then placed in a seated position within an urn of gold for one year while funeral arrangements were finalised.

'*Dieu et mon Droit*' was the battle-cry of Richard I of England to his army at the Battle of Gisors in France. The French were defeated and, in remembrance of this signal victory, Richard made the phrase the motto of the royal arms of England.

George I ate a large meal consisting mainly of melons, got in his coach afterwards and promptly died of apoplexy.

Everything went wrong at the funeral of George II in November 1760. The historian Horace Walpole wrote: 'When we came into the Henry VII Chapel, all solemnity and decorum ceased. No order was observed, people stood or sat where-ever they could or would. The Yeomen of the Guard [carrying the coffin in] were calling out for help, oppressed by the immense weight of their burden, the bishop read sadly and blundered in his prayers, and the anthem, besides being immeasurably tedious, was more fit for a nuptial than a funeral.'

After the honoured guests at the coronation banquet of George IV had finished the repast and departed, the hundreds of spectators in the balconies rushed down and proceeded to eat or steal everything in sight. Food and drink, gold dishes, plates, finger-bowls, napkins and cutlery vanished. One lady pocketed a valuable crested spoon and, when challenged by a court lackey, exclaimed, 'Man, lay a finger on me and I will scream my heart out!' Aware of the dire consequences, he allowed her to leave with the trinket.

After Richard III was defeated by Henry VII at the Battle of Bosworth in 1485, his corpse was buried in Grey Friars Abbey in Leicester, but his bones were later dug up and thrown into the River Soar nearby.

About the year AD 500, the Welsh were so insubordinate and unpolished that a law had to be enacted stating 'that none of the courtiers should give the Queen a blow, or snatch anything with violence out of her hand, under the penalty of forfeiting her Majesty's protection.'

When Henry IV died in 1413 his body was taken by sea to be buried in Canterbury cathedral, but on the way a storm arose; this was blamed on its royal cargo, so the sailors threw it overboard and substituted another body, probably that of a seaman. The substitution remained undiscovered until 1823, when the coffin was opened to reveal human remains clad in ordinary clothes and without the regalia originally placed there.

Henry VI (1422–1461), in one of his more capricious moods, performed a ceremony in which he crowned with his own hands the young Duke of Warwick as 'King of the Isle of Wight'. Commonsense later prevailed and, following Warwick's death, that part of the country ceased to be a kingdom.

The seventeenth-century sultan of Morocco was certainly one for the sultanas and concubines, for during his reign he sired at least 525 sons and 342 daughters.

The Shah of Persia, while visiting Queen Victoria, was also shown around a London prison. On viewing the gallows, he asked for a demonstration; informed that no one was waiting to be hanged, he exclaimed, 'Well, use one of my officials!'

Adolf Frederick, King of Sweden, died in 1771 after a sumptuous banquet of sauerkraut, oysters and lobsters, washed down with champagne.

When Anne Boleyn was confined in the Tower of London prior to her execution, two women were detailed to stay with her and supervise her every move. One was her cousin, Lady Boleyn; the other a Mistress Coffin.

Although Henry IV, who died in 1413, was buried in a royal tomb in Westminster Abbey, a lock of his hair came into the possession of a Victorian collector, Francis Trevelyan Buckland. Whether it had been stolen from the tomb or acquired from the royal barber, or even from the surgeon who embalmed the royal corpse, was never revealed.

During the reign of Elizabeth I some men, in order to emphasise their masculinity, enlarged the size of their nether garments to a ridiculous extent. It is related that 'a certain gentleman, being in the presence of the Queen and her ladies, was invited by Her Majesty to sit down. Unfortunately in doing so, he tore his breeches on a nail, whereupon, to the Queen's intense amusement, a cataract of sawdust began to pour down his leg, and that part of the garment began to reduce considerably in size!'

So great was the hatred felt by many people for Queen Mary, 'Bloody Mary', that a student of science sought to assassinate her by fixing a large magnifying glass on the roof of a house so that the 'fiery rays' would fall on her and kill her when she walked in the gardens of St James' Palace. It didn't work.

Elizabeth of York, wife of Henry VII, gave birth to a daughter, Katherine, in the Tower of London in 1503, and died shortly afterwards. She was then embalmed 'with gums, spices, sweet wine and wax, and swathed in sixty ells of holland cloth, one ell broad [an ell was 45 inches]. Her body was then sered [sealed with wax], the King's plumber closing her in lead, with an epitaph likewise in lead.' The King's plumber wasn't the workman who changed the washers on the royal taps; 'plumber' comes from the Latin *plumbum*, meaning lead.

At the funeral of Queen Charlotte, one of the Yeomen of the Guard carrying the coffin had nearly caused a catastrophe by stumbling. The authorities realised the risk and, at George III's funeral in 1820, the coffin was placed on a trolley, a state-of-the-art mechanical bier covered with a rich pall – which also covered the six Yeomen of the Guard who propelled it.

The largest diamond in the world, the 'Cullinan', weighing 3,025 carats and measuring 4ins × 2ins × 2ins, was found in South Africa in 1905 and presented by that Government to King Edward VII. In order to transport it without risk, a heavily guarded package was delivered to the captain of a liner bound for England; he locked the package in his safe and detectives stayed on board throughout the voyage. The criminal fraternity having being suitably deterred, the diamond was then despatched by ordinary parcel post and reached Buckingham Palace safely.

In an attempt to assassinate Louis Philippe of France on 28 July 1835, a criminal named Fieschi constructed a machine which he set up in a room overlooking the route along which His Majesty would pass. It comprised a large square platform of oak, standing on supports and tilted forward so that the 25 gun barrels mounted on top would point down through the window into the street. A trail of gunpowder led to the guns which, when ignited from a safe distance, would fire them almost simultaneously. The King escaped injury, but 42 spectators were killed or wounded, as were several officers and horses. Fieschi was later caught and guillotined.

If James I had known more about botany, the royal family would have had to find somewhere else to live than Buckingham Palace. Because it was fashionable among early seventeenth-century aristocracy to wear silken garments, James decided that a silkworm factory in the heart of the City would be a highly lucrative venture. Accordingly he had thousands of mulberry trees planted in St James' Park and imported thousands of silkworms, then sat back and waited for them to get eating and spinning. He continued to wait, until he was told that the worms had died of hunger because the mulberries were the black variety, not the white, the leaves of which kept the worms alive and spinning. So the grounds became a promenade for the gallants and ladies of the day until a stately house was built on the site, owned by the Duke of Buckingham. In 1761 the Duke sold Buckingham House to George III for £21,000 and the King renamed it Buckingham Palace. Some of the royal occupants still wear silk, but only ordinary earthworms live in the lawns at the back.

In Durance Vile

The wearing by a convicted criminal of a red letter on an outer garment was compulsory in earlier times in America. In 1656 a woman was not only whipped in two neighbouring towns on market day for blaspheming but was also fined and 'forever in the future to have the Roman "B" cutt out of ridd cloth & sewed to her vper garment on her right arm, in sight.'

Recalcitrant prisoners in America's San Quentin jail in 1937 were punished by what was surely the most inexpensive device ever – just a circle of grey paint, two feet in diameter, on the prison floor, in which the culprit had to stand for four hours, twice a day, without moving, other than for a two-minute toilet break twice a day. So effective was the measure that few inmates re-offended.

A nickname given to policemen by convicts exiled to Australia in the nineteenth century was 'coppers', because it was alleged they would turn anyone in for a penny.

In sixteenth-century Germany prisoners were not released from jail unless they swore a solemn oath that they would not take revenge on the judge, officials or warders.

Convicts transported to Australia in the early 1800s were forbidden to look directly at guards, police officers or women settlers. One who disobeyed received a total of 500 lashes and died a few weeks later.

The 'Oregon Boot' was a heavy device locked around US prisoners' ankles to stop them escaping.

Whips used to punish convicts in the Australian colonies consisted of up to twelve leather thongs, knotted at the ends, attached to a whalebone handle.

In order to quell violent prisoners in London's Pentonville jail in the nineteenth century, cayenne pepper was burned and the smoke blown into their cells.

Most women convicts exiled to Australia in the nineteenth century had to break stones in a quarry, do laundry for local townsfolk, operate the treadmill which brought water from the river and even manufacture nails on the anvils in the prison's blacksmith shop. Disobedience was punished by solitary confinement; failing that, the offender would have her head completely shaved.

Branding irons, bearing different letters at their ends, sizzled in Maryland in the 1600s: SL, for seditious libel, was burned with one letter on each cheek, and M for manslaughter or T for thief on the felon's left hand, as was F for forgery. Burglars had the letter B searing the flesh of their right hand or forehead, and a settler who was rash enough to sell arms, powder and shot to Indians was marked for life with the letter I.

Many prisoners served long sentences in Newgate Gaol, but none longer than John Bernardi, who was confined therein in 1690 and remained for nearly fifty years. He married, his wife lived with him, and they had no fewer than ten children, all born in Newgate.

The treadmill, or tread wheel, was introduced into English prisons in 1818 and later into those of other countries. Resembling a king-size hamster wheel, it consisted of a large hollow cylinder of wood on an iron frame, round the circumference of which was a series of steps about eight inches apart. Some wheels accommodated up to 24 prisoners, who, steadying themselves on the handrails, kept the wheel revolving by walking up the steps as they fell away beneath their feet – to no purpose at all, just 'grinding the wind'.

Prison officers are sometimes called 'screws' (literally a nick-name!), the term originating from a punishment carried out by prisoners on the machine known as the Crank. This was a small paddle-wheel which revolved in a box, turned by a handle. Its rotation was governed by sand or gravel in the box, or by a screw-operated brake which could be tightened by a warder, and the number of revolutions was recorded on a dial. A total of ten thousand turns of the handle was sometimes ordered; as the average speed was one thousand two hundred turns per hour, the continuous eight hours or so needed to complete the task was an exhausting and soul-destroying penalty.

Another name for an American-type straitjacket was a 'San Quentin Overcoat'.

Chloride of lime was once used in English prisons to quell rioting convicts: when it was poured on cell floors, the fumes rendered them helpless.

When the stones of the courtyard in Oxfordshire county jail, on the site of the long-gone Oxford Castle, were dug up in 1782, a complete skeleton was discovered, with chains still secured about its leg bones.

So meagre were the rations provided for those incarcerated in eighteenth century English jails that at Christmas many of the prisoners were allowed out into the local towns, chained together in pairs, one of them carrying a basket or sack for food, the other a box for money.

In 1866 a recent invention, photography, became so popular that murderer Joe Bell not only permitted his photo to be taken in the condemned cell by local newspaper reporters, but insisted on copies being given to members of his family.

The American Revolutionary War, which broke out in 1775, made it impossible for England to deport any more of its convicts to that country, so hundreds of men, women and children were imprisoned instead in the 'hulks', old wooden warships moored in the Thames, the Medway and Portsmouth Harbour, in filthy and appalling conditions. This practice continued even after Australia became available as a destination in 1787.

George Jeffries, at one time Lord Chancellor and Lord Chief Justice of England, was later imprisoned and, while awaiting execution, died in the Bloody Tower in the Tower of London on 19 April 1689.

In Victorian prisons, convicts were not allowed to speak to one another, a 'Law of Silence' that was not abolished until 1898. Except when they were in their cells or at chapel, first offenders were also rendered anonymous to each other by having to wear face masks for the first eighteen months of their sentence; women prisoners had to wear alpaca veils.

In ancient Dresden, Germany, felons guilty of attempted escape had to wear a heavy iron collar around their neck and an iron weight of 21lbs on one ankle.

In the fourteenth century, French lepers were housed in institutions called *lazarettos*. Isolated from their friends and families, they were only allowed out when wearing masks to hide their disease-ravaged faces, and had to ring a bell to warn of their approach. To purchase anything they were forced to point at the article and pull it towards them with a stick; and when speaking to a healthy person they were permitted only to whisper. In western Europe alone there were nineteen thousand *lazarettos* housing those called 'Christ's Poor'.

Around 1650 the English Quaker Anne Audland 'was confined in a filthy place, below ground, with an open sewer running through it, with frogs and toads crawling about the floor. Another Quaker who visited her was also arrested and confined with her, both women not being released until many months later.'

The tradition whereby judges sometimes carry a posy of sweet-smelling flowers originated from the danger of infection in the old prisons all round Europe, where jail fever – typhus – raged and epidemics often proved fatal. In 1730 in Somerset, not only prisoners contracted it but the Lord Chief Baron and his servants, the High Sheriff and his servants, lawyers, barristers and their clerks. At the Old Bailey in 1750 the fatalities included the Lord Mayor, two judges, an alderman, an under-sheriff and fifty others.

The only public lunatic asylum in London in the 1700s was the Hospital of St Mary of Bethlehem, known as 'Bedlam'. It was designed in the style of the Tuileries in France, which so infuriated Louis XIV that he threatened to erect a brothel in Paris looking exactly like St James' Palace. A visit to Bedlam, where the pathetic inmates were kept in cages, was a great attraction. Some inmates were occasionally allowed out to roam the countryside as beggars; they had to wear an identifying badge and were known as 'Tom o' Bedlams'. Similar institutions existed in Europe, the

Lunatics Tower in Vienna being a popular venue for tourists until it was closed down in 1853.

Bilboes were seventeenth-century leg-irons, the word being derived from Bilbao, since such items of restraint were found in captured Spanish galleons.

In Yorkshire, nineteenth-century prisoners were marched from prison to their trial at court sometimes as far as 35 miles, handcuffed and chained by the neck, two by two.

In medieval Civitavecchia, Italy, when escaping prisoners were recaptured, their sentences were restarted and doubled. If their original sentence was for life, they received between one hundred and two hundred lashes per day for the first three days of their new sentence.

In prison the notorious highwayman Dick Turpin was restrained by leg-irons, each consisting of an iron ring 5ins in diameter and 1in. thick; these were connected by long iron shackles to a chain belt worn around his waist, thereby forcing him to shuffle along half-bent, taking the weight of the shackles in his hands. The total weight of the ironmongery was 37lbs.

After a mutiny in the Australian penal colony in 1834 had been brutally quelled, thirteen men were hanged in two days. Since a short rope was used, most of them died by strangulation.

Prison reformer Elizabeth Fry (1780–1845) visited Newgate Gaol and wrote of her horror on finding 'nearly three hundred women crowded together in two wards and two cells, sleeping on the floor without so much as a mat for bedding, and many of them were very nearly naked. Everything was filthy, and the stench was disgusting; every one, even the Governor, was reluctant to go among them.'

A Macabre Miscellany

The underworld's nickname for Newgate Prison in London was 'Ackerman's Hotel', Ackerman being the name of the head turnkey. The site of the prison is now occupied, appropriately enough, by the Central Criminal Court of the Old Bailey.

A popular London attraction in the seventeenth century was the Bridewell in Blackfriars, a prison to which Londoners flocked in their hundreds to watch the prisoners, men and women, being flogged on their bare backs. Each flogging would continue until the President of the Board of Governors brought his hammer down on the bench before him. The room constantly echoed with the pitiful cries of the victims: 'Oh, good Sir Robert, knock! Pray, good Sir Robert, please knock!'

While imprisoned in the Tower of London on the orders of James I, Sir Walter Raleigh tried to commit suicide by stabbing himself in the heart, but the blade was deflected by striking one of his ribs.

John Howard, the prison reformer, visited the jail in Hanover, Germany, in 1778 and reported that a felon was interrogated at two o'clock in the morning with the infamous 'Osnabrug Torture', part of which consisted of the executioner tearing the hair from the victim's head, breast and other parts until he confessed. Then he was executed by the sword.

In eighteenth-century Venice, convicts were restrained by 27lbs of fetters and handcuffs, but in Civitavecchia the weight of their leg-irons was gradually decreased year by year as the date of their release approached.

Prisoners in Liège – at that time, the 1770s, in Germany – were incarcerated in cages within prison rooms, the cages being 7ft by 6ft 9ins, and 6ft 6ins high; on one side was an aperture, 6ins by 4ins, through which food was passed.

Prisoners in Antwerp – in the eighteenth century a city in Austrian Flanders – suffered an ingenious torment by being chained in the middle of a room, the floor of which consisted of narrow pieces of wood, four inches apart, laid vertically; the victim was denied shoes and stockings, so that standing or lying down on the edges proved painful in the extreme.

In the German torture *Aufziehen* the victim's arms were tied behind his back, then a rope around his wrists was passed over a pulley and tightened, hoisting him off his feet and inflicting unbearable pain on his shoulder blades; to increase the agony, weights were sometimes attached to his ankles.

John Howard, the prison reformer, was in favour of abolition of the death sentence; instead he advocated life imprisonment with repetitive and periodical floggings.

In 1858 Simon Moore, a normally strong and fit convict in Auburn State Prison, New York, was punished for a minor offence by being kept under a running shower for over half an hour; he died shortly afterwards.

It was reported in 1916 that prisoners who attempted to escape from Onondago County Penitentiary, New York, had chains weighing up to 16lbs riveted to their ankles, which were worn day and night.

A German instrument of torture used in the Middle Ages was the 'Spiked Hare'; far from being a savoury dish, it was a wooden roller fitted with razor-sharp spikes, placed under the back of a victim being racked.

Among the attempts made by prisoners to escape from Sing Sing prison in the 1900s was one in which the inmate made two rubber ducks connected by a length of tubing to a headpiece of the same material; wearing the latter he climbed over the fence, dropped into the Hudson River, swam along underneath his ducks and got clean away, although he was later recaptured.

Newgate Prison, was rebuilt in 1422 with funds bequeathed by Sir Richard Whittington – Dick Whittington – and so condemned prisoners were said 'to have studied at Whittington College, been examined at the Old Bailey, and taken a high degree at Hyde Park Corner [i.e., Tyburn].'

Strict precautions were taken in the 1900s to prevent American prisoners condemned to death from committing suicide: their clothes were made of a material impossible to unpick and make into a rope; they were shaved by a warder; and to prevent them opening an artery with a sharp fingernail, prisoners had to extend their arms through an aperture in the cell door and a warder would wield the nail-clippers.

Lewis E. Lawes, Warden of Sing Sing prison, New York, in 1920, described the case of a prisoner, half Mexican, half African, who asked for a certain black minister to visit him. The minister arrived, togged out in a stovepipe hat and long-tailed coat and, upon being searched, was found to be carrying a heavy .45 Colt pistol. As it turned out, he might have needed it, for the prisoner attacked both the minister and the principal keeper. Mr Lawes reported that the man resisted to the end and died with a curse on his lips.

No fewer than 25 life sentences were passed on Juan Corona in 1971 for the multiple murders of migrant workers that he carried out at his Californian ranch in the 1960s. Fate caught up with him in prison when, two years later, a fight in his cell resulted in him being stabbed 32 times and blinded in one eye.

Private madhouses flourished in London in the 1700s, institutions in which patients were treated with appalling cruelty; one reported incident concerned an inmate who, having managed to escape, ran down the road towards Aldgate dragging behind him the bedhead to which he had been chained.

London's Westminster Cathedral was built between 1895 and 1903 on the site of the notorious Tothill Fields Prison.

Accused in 1278 of counterfeiting, clipping and adulterating the King's coinage, six hundred Jews were imprisoned in the Tower of London. More than two hundred of them, men and women, were hanged in various parts of the city, and many others were banished from the kingdom.

It's hard to imagine anything more calculated to spoil one's appetite than one's impending execution, but an American criminal condemned to die in the electric chair in the 1920s chose, for his last meal, one Long Island duck, one can of peas and one pint of olives, all mixed into a stew with dumplings; also four slices of bread, boiled rice, tomato salad, strawberry shortcake, a pint of vanilla ice cream, and some good cigars. After the banquet, he announced, 'I'm ready to ride that thunderbolt now, boys!'

The 'Spanish Mantle' was used in Denmark and Germany as a punishment in earlier centuries; similar to the 'Drunkard's Cloak', it consisted of a heavy vest resembling a tub, with an aperture for the head and fitted with irons to secure the neck. The Berlin model measured 20ins in diameter at the top, 33ins at the base and 33ins high, and had to be worn for the length of time specified by the magistrate.

MILITARY MAYHEM

Army Regulations introduced in 1914 permitted provost marshals to punish offenders with up to 30 strokes of the lash for some crimes. Soldiers of the Indian Army serving in Iraq in 1917 were disciplined in this manner for attempted desertion.

During World War II thousands of Spaniards joined Hitler's armies fighting on the Eastern Front. Many, having been captured in battle, were stripped, mutilated and transfixed to the ground by Russian bayonets.

In 1745 five soldiers involved in the Jacobite Uprising were marched to Hyde Park to be executed. The wife of one of them threw herself at her husband's feet, crying bitterly, 'Surely they do not mean to shoot my William – the King has not such men in his army as would do that!' Shortly after the firing squad had done its work, the woman's body was rescued from the nearby New River – alas, too late.

When sentenced to the army's 'Picquet' punishment, a soldier's wrists were tied to a ceiling hook and his weight was taken by one foot resting on a sharp spike in the floor.

In 1743 Scottish soldiers found guilty of mutiny were shot by firing squad within the Tower of London. Today thousands of tourists unwittingly walk over their graves.

A military punishment administered in the armed forces of many countries was 'Running the Gauntlet' (originally, Gantlope). In 1676 in New York the sentence passed on a soldier guilty of pilfering stated: 'The Court Marshall doth adjudge that the said Melchior Classen shall run the Gantlope once, the length of the fort where, according to custom, the souldiers shall have switches with which they shall strike him as he passes between them stript to the waist, and at the Fort-gate the Marshall is to receive him and there kick him out of the garrison as a cashiered person, when he is no more to return, and if any pay is due him, it is to be forfeited.'

Wrongdoers among American Civil War soldiers were sentenced to be chained by the ankle to a log of wood, a 'clog', often for long periods. One offender, caught stealing firewood, was made 'to wear a clogg for four days and wear his coat rong side turn'd out'.

At the Battle of Trafalgar on 21 October 1805 Admiral Nelson was seriously wounded when a musket ball fired by a French sniper, Sergeant Robert Guillemard, penetrated his chest. 'They have done for me, Hardy,' he exclaimed to his captain. 'My backbone is shot through.' Later, realising he was dying, he said, 'Don't throw me over-board.' He was assured on this score, and it is said that on the homeward journey his body was preserved in a barrel of rum.

In 1757 a British naval officer, Admiral Byng, having been found guilty of negligence in battle, was shot by firing squad on board a warship in Portsmouth Harbour.

The seventeenth-century military punishment for blasphemy was to have one's tongue bored through with a red-hot iron.

In 1756 the Indians rebelled and captured many English settlers and soldiers, 146 of them being imprisoned in a small hut 'crammed together in a cube of 18ft'. In oppressive heat, without food, water or access to fresh air, the prisoners suffered terribly, and the next morning only 23 of them staggered out of the 'Black Hole of Calcutta'.

In the Reform riots at Peterloo in Manchester in 1819 the cavalry charged in an attempt to disperse the crowds. As described by a contemporary, 'They evidently could not, with all the weight of man and horse, penetrate that compact mass of human beings, and their sabres were plied to hew a way through naked, held-up hands and defenceless heads; and then chopped limbs and would-gaping skulls were seen, and groans and screams, mingled with the din of confusion, came from the crowd-moiled and sabre-doomed who could not escape.'

In order to select the body of the Unknown Soldier in Westminster Abbey, six corpses of unknown servicemen were taken from various sectors of the World War I battlefront. They were placed in identical coffins, each covered by the Union Jack, and a general was then asked to lay his hand on one of them. The other five were buried in France, while the chosen one was taken to London, where, on a gun carriage, it rested in Whitehall while King George V unveiled the Cenotaph. The coffin was then buried in the Abbey with full honours.

The gas shells fired by the Germans during World War I caused victims to panic as they desperately tried to breathe; their tongues swelled and their faces turned purple, and death overtook hundreds of them.

Sailors being 'flogged round the Fleet' were whipped while sailing slowly in a small boat past the other ships, the crews of which had to line the rails and watch, as a warning.

When the nineteenth-century army surgeon James Barry died, those preparing the body for burial were surprised when 'he' turned out to be a 'she'.

After annihilating the French Mediterranean Fleet in 1707 Admiral Sir Cloudesley Shovel, commander of the English fleet, sailed for home, but his ship sank in a storm off the Isles of Scilly. The admiral's battered, bruised but still breathing body was washed up on the shore, where it was found by a fisherman's wife who, coveting the emerald ring on his finger, promptly killed him. She kept her grim secret until confessing it to a clergyman before she died thirty years later; he then passed the ring on to Shovel's old friend, the Earl of Berkeley.

When the pirate Blackbeard, Edward Teach, was killed in a hand-to-hand fight with Royal Navy Lieutenant Maynard, his victorious opponent sailed home with Blackbeard's head hanging from his ship's bowsprit.

The tradition among primitive tribes of taking trophies from their beaten enemies was still maintained in northwest Africa when, in 1824, Sir Charles McCarthy, governor of the province, sought to quell a local uprising. His force of six hundred British soldiers was vastly outnumbered by the Ashantee tribesmen and, under attack, he ordered the band to play the National Anthem again and again to keep his men's spirits high. But worse was to follow, for when crates that were believed to be full of ammunition were opened, they were found to contain only army biscuits! Defeated, those who survived were decapitated by the enemy, including Sir Charles. But so impressed were the Ashantees by his leadership that after sawing off the dome of his skull they decorated it with jewels and gold bands and used it as a ceremonial cup, hoping thereby to acquire some of his bravery.

The superstition that it is bad luck to light three cigarettes with one match is well known. It is said to have originated in World War I, when the lighting of the first cigarette alerted an enemy sniper, the second allowed him to take aim and the third was his opportunity to fire. The *Weekly Despatch* in October 1920 carried an account of one match being used to light the cigars of King Alexander of Greece, his aide and the captain of the ship they were visiting. Jokingly, His Majesty referred to the superstition, adding, 'Before the end of the year, one of us three is doomed to die.' His words were prophetic, for a few days later he was bitten by a diseased monkey – and died.

During the Russian Revolution many atrocities were committed by both sides. It was reported in 1919 that officers taken prisoner by the Bolsheviks had their shoulder straps nailed to their shoulders.

Mines were used during World War II to blow up tanks, armoured personnel carriers and similar vehicles – but never wheelchairs. Such an explosive device, however, had been attached to one in which Archibald Brown was seated, in 1943, and without warning it suddenly exploded, killing him instantly and scattering his body parts over a wide area. The murderer proved to be his son who, diagnosed as schizophrenic, was declared guilty but insane.

After winning the Battle of Waterloo in 1815, the Duke of Wellington was appointed to take charge of the army of occupation in Paris. At one reception the French generals present showed their animosity towards him by turning their backs on him, and, when Louis XIII apologised for their discourtesy, Wellington reassured him, exclaiming, 'Do not distress yourself, Sire. They've got so in the habit of showing me their backs that they can't get out of it!'

The seemingly innocuous order by General Jos. Valdes during the 1930s Spanish Civil War that a prisoner be given some coffee was not a sign of his benevolence towards the victim but was a euphemism for proceeding with the execution.

Even on the battlefield one had to look after one's complexion and appearance. An advertisement appeared during the Seven Years War for 'Campaign boxes for officers, fitted with eau-de-luc, rouge, perfumed pomatum, powder puffs, lip salve and ivory eye-brow combs'.

The legend of 'Drake's Drum', that the famous admiral would return and fight for his country on hearing the instrument being beaten, is well known. The story was revived in 1918 when some of the German fleet surrendered to the British; as they did so, drum rolls were heard throughout the flagship. Exhaustive efforts were made to locate the sound, but without success, every seaman on board being found at his post.

Following the capture of Royalist-held Drogheda in Ireland by Cromwell's forces in 1649, three thousand of the inhabitants were massacred.

In bygone days officers wore metal epaulettes on their shoulders to protect them from sabre blows deflected by their helmets; in more modern times epaulettes displayed the ranks of officers. However, in the Far East campaign during World War II, they indicated to Japanese snipers exactly whom to aim at, so badges of rank were subsequently transferred to less conspicuous places on the uniform.

The punishment of a soldier by giving him 150 lashes roused the public's anger so much that in 1846 it was announced that in future the maximum would be 50 lashes, although some

Members of Parliament argued that if flogging were ever abolished altogether, the high state of discipline, of which the British Army was so justly proud, might be lost.

During the Seven Years War with France it was necessary to capture the enemy stronghold of Belleisle, and ten thousand troops were transported to attack the island. But the siege lasted much longer than expected, for the ingenious French governor, desperately short of defenders, doubled the apparent size of his garrison by dressing all the women of the island in bright red uniforms like those of the soldiers, and having them gallop round the ramparts; because he was similarly short of horses, he had some of the women mounted on equally capable but less frisky cows.

Strange things happen on the battlefield. In the celebrated charge of the Light Brigade at Balaclava, Captain Nolan, who had just brought the fatal order to Lord Lucan to charge the Russian guns, was struck by a shell 'which buried itself in his heart'. The sword fell from his hand but his arm remained uplifted and his knees still gripped the saddle, and not until the frightened horse had galloped through the Light Dragoons in the first line did his corpse fall to the ground. A similar instance occurred when a Southern soldier in the American Civil War was shot just as he was mounting his horse; he stood there fixed, one foot in the stirrup, the other on the ground; his horse had not moved on. And a French soldier at the Battle of Sedan, killed by the explosion of a shell just as he was raising a cup to his lips, kept his hand raised – even though his head had been blown away.

Until the end of the nineteenth century a punishment inflicted by the French navy was *La Cale*. It consisted of hoisting the wrongdoer to a considerable height from the yard-arm and then letting him fall; if sentenced to *Cale Sèche* he fell on the deck, if to *Cale Humide*, he fell into the sea.

At the brutal attack on Drogheda, by Cromwell's forces, the garrison was commanded by Sir Arthur Ashton who, it was rumoured, had a wooden leg full of gold coins. After he had been killed, the Roundhead soldiers, much to their regret, found it to be solid timber. Instead, all the gold, two hundred broad pieces, had been sewn in his belt, and minor fights broke out as the men cut it to ribbons.

After the Battle of Trafalgar, the Duke of Wellington advanced into France, but found it almost impossible to purchase essential supplies from the French peasants, because of the lack of French currency. Never daunted, His Lordship issued an order calling for any soldiers among the British ranks whose criminal past included coining (illegally melting down coins in order to manufacture those of a higher denomination) to come forward, promising them indemnity if they did so; he then put them to work turning English sovereigns into *napoléons* and *louis d'or*.

Between 1902 and 1941 hundreds of men died in wartime leaving daughters who became orphans. The girls were taken into care by various London orphanages and, on their deaths, most were buried in the graveyard of St John-at-Hampstead Church, each gravestone bearing the girl's name and the regimental details of her father; the area was further enhanced by the 'Soldiers' Daughters' monument.

Little reverence was shown to the sanctity of St Paul's Cathedral during Cromwellian times: although part of it became a Puritan chapel, a much larger area was occupied by eight hundred of the Protector's dragoons and their horses.

TRADITIONS AND SUPERSTITIONS

A custom among early American Indians to hasten a woman's labour was to take her on to the prairie; there a horseman would ride at her as if intending to run her down; but turn aside at the very last moment. The fear so induced was apparently effective in shortening her labour.

The saying 'one for the road' is believed to have originated with the practice whereby the procession to Tyburn gallows would halt to allow the condemned felon to have a last drink.

An old legend stated that should a raven perch on a house in which a person was ill, the invalid would surely die, the bird's harsh cry of 'caw, caw' being said to resemble the words 'corpse, corpse!'

In the Middle Ages a 'Hand of Glory' carried by burglars was believed to cause the residents of a house to remain asleep while being robbed. It consisted of the hand of a hanged man or unborn baby, suitably dried, the fingers bent to support a candle made of the 'recipient's' fat, the wick consisting of strands of their hair. Its power was invoked by the reciting of the Lord's Prayer backwards.

In medieval Nuremberg, if a condemned man had died or committed suicide, his fettered corpse was brought into court and asked to produce an advocate; being unable to answer, he would be declared officially dead. An advocate would then be appointed, who would attempt to prove his client's innocence. This gruesome practice was discontinued in 1526.

The ominous phrase 'gone west' probably dates from the time when condemned men were taken westwards from the Tower to Tyburn gallows.

When the Northern Lights (Aurora Borealis) are seen south of the Arctic Circle, many believe them to be an evil omen. Some months before the outbreak of World War II they were sighted by London residents, and in 1941, just prior to the Japanese attack on Pearl Harbor, Americans living as far south as Ohio reported seeing the Aurora in all its glory.

As an alternative to being used for dissection, the corpses of eighteenth century Scottish prisoners were sometimes hanged in chains, the court's sentence including the blood-chilling phrases 'until the birds of the air pick the flesh off your body, and your bones bleach and whiten in the winds of heaven, as a constant warning to all.'

The original name of the Bloody Tower in the Tower of London was the Garden Tower, because of the gardens which once adjoined it.

In Switzerland every eighteenth-century seigneurie of a canton, or lord of the manor, had the power to judge, condemn and capitally convict criminals; both men and women offenders were beheaded by the sword.

Until as recently as the end of the nineteenth century, people believed that the souls of those who have passed on dwell in the flowers of the broad bean. This ancient tradition originated in

Roman days, when those attending funerals partook of them as part of the mourning meals.

When epidemics of leprosy swept England in the Middle Ages, it was believed that a certain cure would be forthcoming if the sufferers stood beneath a gallows and allowed the cadavers' blood to drip on them.

Under the 'law of the bier' a murder suspect would be forced to touch the corpse; if he or she were guilty, the corpse would start to bleed.

In the Middle Ages 'unicorn's horn' was extremely expensive. Because it was believed capable of destroying poisons in food, it was much sought after by European royalty; French monarchs dipped a piece of it into a goblet before drinking. The belief continued until Charles II's reign, when the Royal Society declared it to have no antidote properties whatsoever. The Americans were also taken in by its allegedly remarkable powers; Governor Endicott lent one to Governor John Winthrop for his medical practice. The 'unicorn' was probably the narwhal, and the horn ordinary ivory.

A custom without legal foundation existed in earlier years that a man could sell his wife – with her consent – by leading her to the market-place by a cord around her neck, the only proviso being that she could not be sold for less than a shilling (5p). Once bought, she became her new 'owner's' wife and the seller could then marry again. The Annual Record of 1832 reported that a man put his wife up for sale in Carlisle but warned prospective buyers that for three years she had been a domestic curse to him; nevertheless he swapped her for twenty shillings and a dog! And in 1881 a woman accused of bigamy swore she had been 'legally' sold by her first husband – and even produced a stamped receipt.

The word 'silly' originally applied to people who were happy or blessed, rather than, as now, stupid or inane. The people who were to be avoided were those who were cross-eyed and would therefore bring bad luck to mariners, bull-fighters and those in similarly hazardous professions.

Albatrosses were believed to possess the souls of dead seamen – a superstition highly relevant to the case of the SS *Calpean Star* in 1939. The troubles encountered by that ship were attributed by the crew to the fact that one such bird formed part of the cargo, bound for a German zoo; when the bird was found to be dead on arrival, fifty of the crew refused to continue sailing with the ship.

In Eastern Europe it was believed that unless a newly-built structure incorporated a living being in the foundations, it would soon collapse. When human sacrifices became unobtainable, the only alternative was for one workman to engage a passer-by in conversation while another surreptitiously measured the man's shadow with a length of string, which was then buried in the foundations.

In May 1878 murderer Eugène-Marie Chantrelle was invited to choose his last meal before facing the gallows. With typical French verve he asked for two bottles of champagne and a woman; with typical English verve his request was denied.

When Swedish spinsters were buried, it was customary to include a mirror with any personal belongings in the coffin, so that they could smarten their appearance ready for Judgment Day. This facility was not required by married ladies, who, as a symbol of wedlock, always wore their hair combed and pinned up.

The presence of a corpse aboard ship is always viewed with apprehension by the crew, but their superstitious anxiety is lessened if the cadaver lies athwart, that is, across the width of the ship, rather than along its length. On arrival in port it is essential that the body be carried on to the dockside before anyone else disembarks.

When someone dies it is essential that his or her eyes are closed; if not, tradition has it that, until their interment, the dead person will continue to look for someone to accompany them to the grave.

In England and parts of France it was believed that when a man was buried, he became the churchyard watcher, with the job of calling upon the next man doomed to die, who would then take over the phantom chore. In Ireland and Scotland this often resulted in a desperate race if two funeral parties approached the cemetery at the same time, the horses being whipped up to avoid their passenger being burdened with that awesome task instead of being allowed to 'rest in peace'. Should a cemetery eventually be closed, the last man interred therein would perforce perform the watcher's duties for eternity.

Anyone passing a graveyard at night should be reminded of the need to look out for a small flame hovering over a grave, which signifies the presence of a soul unable to rest. Icelandic sagas frequently referred to such emanations, describing them as the souls of their warriors guarding the treasures interred with them.

Those abiding by an ancient Middle Eastern tradition believed that minor ailments such as toothache or headache could be remedied by the possession of a nail from a gallows; acquiring one for that purpose was one of the few activities permitted on a holy day.

In medieval Scotland the laird had absolute power over the peasants on his estate, even the right to deflower local girls on their wedding night. To thwart him, many young women got pregnant first, then got married.

An ancient tradition states that in order to ensure a happy marriage the bridal procession should never pass through the lych-gate of a church but find some other way of entering. The reason is that the word 'lych' means 'corpse', and the lych-gate was where the coffin bearers would rest their burden before carrying it into the church.

Primitive man believed that when he looked into a pool or lake, what he saw was not his reflection but his soul. Nowadays mirrors are used to inspect one's appearance, but should there be no reflection, it means that death is approaching and one's soul has gone on ahead.

People were, and some still are, wary of a man whose eyebrows meet, considering him sinister and untrustworthy. Greeks used to suspect them of being vampires, while Germans and Danes thought they were werewolves; an old Icelandic name for one possessing such hirsutely conjoined brows was *hamrammr*, meaning, able to change their body-shape at will.

The ancient remedy for aching joints, rheumatism and the like was to wear what was known as a cramp ring, preferably one made from the iron parts of a coffin – the handles, hinges or nails.

Yeoman Warders of the Tower of London and Yeomen of the Guard were compelled to be bearded, a ruling that was not ... until 1936, by order of Edward VIII. Many opt out – the ...

... it was believed that some rivers had their own ... in the waters, with the right to possess the body of anyone who fell in; in some cases, bystanders would ignore cries for help and just walk on. A case was reported in 1904 of a man who fell into the river Derwent in Derbyshire. A local who witnessed the tragedy referred to the river as a person, explaining, 'He said Derwent was nought but a brook, but Derwent got 'im. They never saw his head, he threw up his arms, but Derwent wouldn't let 'im go. Ay, it's a sad pity, he had seven children, but he shouldn't ha made so light o' Derwent.'

It was an old custom in the Western world that, when a person dies, all the doors and windows should be left open, for their soul to leave; and that mirrors in the room should be covered over, in the belief that should anyone look into them and see the dead person looking back at them, their own death would soon occur.

A Venetian visiting England in the early 1500s was greatly surprised at the amount of promiscuous kissing that went on. 'Everybody kisses everybody else,' he wrote. 'What is really pleasant is that you are expected to kiss the ladies, be they married or single, after you have been once formally presented to them, where-ever you meet them. This is very agreeable when the ladies are young and fair, but otherwise . . .'

Some countries in the Middle Ages believed that animals were responsible for their actions; at Falaise in 1386, a sow injured a child, causing it to die, so the animal was dressed in men's clothing and publicly hanged.

In Elizabeth I's time, many German workers engaged in melting down and refining coins in the Royal Mint, then based in the Tower of London, fell ill from inhaling the fumes. They were advised that drinking from a dead man's skull would cure and so those in charge of the Mint negotiated with the London Bridge authorities 'to take of the headds uppon the Bridge and make cuppes thereof, whereof they dranke and founde some relief.' It didn't work, though, because 'the mooste of them dyed.'

It was the practice in former times for Chinese women, when young, to bind their feet tightly. This was believed to have been introduced in about AD 580 by Emperor Chen-Hon-Djon, who considered that it added to their feminine charm, although walking when one's feet were only four inches in length must have been difficult in the extreme.

Copper bracelets are widely advertised to guard against various maladies such as cramp, but for real relief, as practised in the nineteenth century, you can't beat keeping the feet of a mole in your pocket. To remember which particular feet to employ is easy: should the arms or shoulders be rheumatic, the 'arms', or front feet, of the mole are needed; if the hips or legs, the back feet will do the trick. And if you've got warts, just let the blood of a freshly killed mole drip on them.

A dire warning to dressmakers and tailors: once pins have been used in making a shroud or coffin lining, never use them again on clothing for the living. Even if removed from grave clothes, the pins should always be placed, loose if necessary, in the coffin with the corpse.

A rainbow is not simply a meteorological phenomenon; traditionally it is the Lord's sign in the sky, a declaration that the earth will never be inundated by the rains as it was during the Flood. Indians and Finns swear that the rainbow was the weapon by which lightning bolts were fired at the god of thunder; in Scandinavia it was the soul bridge between man and the gods, a belief also found in Germany and Austria, where it was thought to be the route to heaven taken by children, escorted by their guardian angels.

The legend that if the ravens leave the Tower of London, the realm will collapse and the country be conquered was first mentioned in Henry VIII's time, but it originated with the Celtic god Bran the Blessed, who, mortally wounded in battle, ordered his head to be cut off and buried in the White Mount (now Tower Hill) facing France. As long as his head remained there, he said, England would never be invaded. The significance of this legend is that *Bran* is Celtic for 'raven'.

Men wearing suits or blazers are unwittingly prepared for sword play. The two or three small buttons at the cuffs of their jacket sleeves originate in the days when, before a duel, the fashionably long, lacy shirt sleeves which almost covered the duellists' hands were drawn back out of the way and buttoned to those of the outer garment.

Electrical discharge hovering around the riggings of ships at sea is known as St Elmo's Fire, named after the patron saint of Mediterranean mariners, who perished in that ocean during a violent storm. A naval tradition is that it is the ghostly spirit of a drowned shipmate and should never be approached or touched, on pain of death.

The mandrake plant was long regarded with fear and wonder, mainly because its shape resembles that of a tiny human being. It was much sought after for medicinal purposes by herbalists in the Middle Ages, but it was reputed that when pulled up, the miniature 'creature' would utter screams so terrifying that anyone hearing them would instantly go mad and die. An ancient solution was for the herbalist to fill his ears with wax, loosen the soil around the plant and, after tying one end of a cord to the plant, attach the other to a dog. A sharp blow with a stick to the rear of the animal would extract the plant, yielding one valuable mandrake – and one dead dog.

A funeral in the 1670s, as described by a contemporary historian, was quite a macabre procedure. 'Male corpses wore caps, but female corpses wore a Kind of Head-Dress, with a Fore-head-cloth. The body being thus equipped and laid in the Coffin, They let it lye three or four Days in this Condition; which Time they allow, as well as to give the dead Person an Opportunity of coming to Life again, if his Soul has not quite left his Body, as to prepare Mourning, and the Ceremonies of the Funeral. They send the Beadle (a parish official) with a List of such Friends and Relations as they have a Mind to invite; and sometimes they have printed Tickets which they deliver. A little before the Company is due to arrive, they lay the Body into the Coffin upon two Stools, in a Room, where all that please may go and see it; then they take off the Top of the Coffin and remove from off the Face a little square Piece of Flannel, made on Purpose to cover it, and not fastened to any Thing. The Relations and chief Mourners are in a Chamber apart, with their more intimate Friends; and the rest of the Guests are dispersed in several Rooms about the House. When they are ready to set out, they nail up the Coffin, and a Servant presents the Company with Sprigs of Rosemary; Every one takes a Sprig and carries it in his Hand 'til the Body is put into the Grave, at which Time they throw their Sprigs in after it. Before They set out, and after They return, it is usual to present the Guests with something to drink, either white or red Wine, boil'd with Sugar and Cinnamon, or some other such Liquor. Everyone drinks two or three Cups. Note; No Men ever go to Womens Burials, nor the Women to the Mens.'

Scotland's thistle emblem is traditionally believed to have originated at the time of the Danish invasion; approaching by night, silently and bare-footed, one Dane unfortunately stepped on a thistle, and his yelp of pain – doubtless accompanied by a suitable expletive – gave warning to the Scots, who then attacked and slaughtered their foes.

A belief still held in some countries is that one's shadow is one's soul; deliberate injury to it could result in injury or death to its 'owner'. An Irish legend described how Fionn killed his enemy Cuirrech by repeatedly stabbing his shadow.

Following the death of a pope in the Middle Ages, not only were his apartments denuded of valuables, but the very corpse itself was deprived of rings and similar religious items by his relatives. Aimon, author of *Tableau de la Cour de Rome*, wrote: 'When a pope is in his last extremity, his nephews and servants carry from the palace all they can find. Immediately after his death the officers of the Apostolic Chamber strip the body of everything valuable, but the relations of the pope generally forestall them, and with such promptitude that nothing remains but the bare walls and the body, placed on an old mattress, with an old wooden candlestick and a wax end in it.'

A large blue gravestone in Westminster Abbey called 'Long Meg' is believed to cover the remains of 26 monks of the Abbey who died of the Black Death in 1348. Others hold that it is the burial place of a famous giantess, 'Long Meg of Westminster', who lived during the reign of Henry VIII.

An ancient superstition declared that to guard against evil spirits, if a baby was taken into a stranger's house before it had been christened, salt should be put into its mouth and a piece of coral hung around its neck.

In the Middle Ages material from Egyptian mummies was used as a potent remedy for bruises and abrasions. Francis I always carried with him a little packet of mummy and rhubarb for falls and other accidents.

In earlier days anyone was allowed to sit in the Coronation Chair in Westminster Abbey on payment of a small fee to the vergers; this resulted in names and dates being carved all over it, one being 'P. Abbott slept in this chair 5.6. July 1800' (no relation to the author, I hasten to add!). During World War II it was taken to a place of safety in Gloucester and the Coronation Stone, removed from it, was secretly buried within the Abbey. In the event of the building being bombed or the country invaded by the enemy, the details of the Stone's location were deposited with the Office of the Prime Minister of Canada.

A traditional Scottish custom once existed whereby, should the jury have found a prisoner guilty, the judge would symbolise the snuffing out of a life by extinguishing a lighted candle before pronouncing the death sentence.

Entertainments such as cock fighting and bear baiting were all the rage in the seventeenth and eighteenth centuries, although one that took place in a hall situated in what is now Ray Street, Clerkenwell, was dangerous in the extreme, for it featured 'a mad bull, with fireworks attached to its horns and body, being let loose among the men present, together with a dog also adorned with fireworks, and a bear with a cat tied to its tail.'

A novel cure for those with troublesome indigestion is to keep the front right foot of a hare in one's pocket. The efficacy of this was vouched for by Samuel Pepys, who wrote in his *Diary* for 25 March 1665, 'Now I am at a losse to know whether it be my hare's foot which is my preservative against wind, for I never had a fit of the colique since I wore it.'

A MACABRE MISCELLANY

Other than the working classes, most people powdered their hair with wheaten flour in the eighteenth century. The army in 1795 had 150,000 men, and allowing a pound of powder a week per man, this totalled 22,800,000 lbs annually. If the army in Ireland and India is included, the total reaches 250,000 lbs a week, or 650 tons per year – enough to make 3,059,353 quartern loaves, sufficient to feed 50,000 people with bread for twelve months.

WITCH WAY TO DIE

Joan of Arc, heroine of France, led an army of supporters against the English in 1429, but two years later, her hands and feet manacled, she was taken in a cage to Rouen Castle, where she faced trial for witchcraft. Although only nineteen years old, she was found guilty and burned at the stake in the town's market place. The executioner afterwards disembowelled her remains and threw her half-incinerated heart and organs into the River Seine.

It was believed that garlic worn as a necklace, or scissors left open in the shape of a cross and buried beneath the doorway of a house, provided protection against witches.

In earlier centuries, evidence that a woman was a witch was obtained by 'swimming' her. She was stripped naked, her left thumb bound to her right big toe and her right thumb to her left big toe, and immersed in the village pond. If she floated, it proved that the Devil was supporting her; if she sank, she was innocent – although she was not always rescued in time.

In medieval times official witchfinders used long needles to locate the 'Devil's Mark' – any small area of a woman's naked and shaven body insensitive to pain – and, on doing so, denounced her as a witch.

As an alternative to ducking a woman suspected of being a witch, she would be stripped to her shift (petticoat) and weighed against the church Bible; if lighter, she would be burned at the stake.

A Macabre Miscellany

Professing to be a sorcerer, Herman Billik gained influence over Martin Vzral, his wife and five children in order to extract money from them. During the following two years, 1905–06, Martin and three of the children died horrific deaths, their life insurances being collected by the sorrowing mother and Billik. When arsenic was discovered in their bodies, the police visited Mrs Vzral, only to find that she had committed suicide. Billik was put on trial and sentenced to life imprisonment in a US penitentiary.

During the year 1591 in the German town of Ellingen, 72 women were accused of being witches and were consequently hanged or burned to death.

Witchcraft was rife in Ireland in earlier centuries. During building work in 1968, excavations uncovered the skeleton of a small boy having a larger skull than normal; it was believed to be that of an eighteenth-century Black Mass sacrifice.

An old tradition stated that a spell cast by a witch could be broken by causing her face to bleed above the level of her mouth and nose. This was evidently believed by a farmer who, as reported by a national newspaper, thinking that a neighbour had bewitched some of his cattle, tried but failed to scratch her forehead with a pin.

Most horrific murders are eventually solved, even though many years may elapse before the criminal is finally arrested, but a case still remaining on police files in Scotland Yard is that of Charles Walton, whose body was discovered in a Warwickshire field in 1945. He had been put to death in an unmistakeably occult manner: he was found lying on his back, pinned to the ground with a pitchfork through his neck, and with a billhook, which had been used to carve a deep wound in the shape of a cross in his throat and chest, protruding obscenely from his ribcage.

Shakespeare's *Macbeth* is viewed by actors as a very unlucky play; indeed, some will not mention it by name but refer to it only as 'that play' or 'the Scottish play'. It's believed that the 'Witches' Song' in the play contains strange powers of evil.

After a series of witchcraft trials in Sweden in 1669, not only were 85 adults beheaded and their corpses burned, but 36 of their children received beatings over several months.

Even as recently as 1956, a Mexican woman, Josefina Arista, was accused of witchcraft and burned at the stake, her ashes then being scattered in the wind.

Philippe Auguste of France ruled that not only witches and sorcerers should be put to death by drowning, but also 'untitled' people who swore!

The word 'God' was anathema to witches and so, when one man finally persuaded his wife, a practising witch, to allow him to accompany her to a sabbat, or witches' get-together, she agreed on condition that he didn't mention the names of any Christian deities. When the assembly sat down to a feast, the man asked for the salt and, on eventually receiving it, exclaimed 'God be praised!' Next minute, as recorded by Paulus, a sixteenth-century Italian, he found himself alone, miles from anywhere. He was so disgusted with the treatment he had received that when he got home he promptly reported his wife to the Inquisition and had her burned to death.

Throughout Europe, one way of ridding oneself of an enemy was to manufacture a small waxen image, preferably incorporating some of their hair or nail clippings. The gradual melting of the figure in a fire would guarantee the slow and painful death of the quarry. One such image, of a woman dressed in a bonnet and gown, was found when building repairs were carried out in a Hereford Council office in January 1960. Adhering to the dusty and crumpled material of the dress was a note bearing the name Mary Ann Wand, which read: 'I act this spell upon you from my whole heart, wishing you to never rest nor eat nor sleep the restern part of your life. I hope your flesh will waste away and I hope you will never spend another penny I ought to have. Wishing you this from my whole heart.' One wonders what Mary Ann had done to deserve all that!

STRANGE AND SINGULAR

William Laud, Archbishop of Canterbury, was found guilty of high treason and beheaded in 1645. His pet tortoise continued to live in Ely Palace for the next 108 years, and would have lived even longer had not a clumsy servant stepped on it in 1753.

The time taken to reduce the average adult corpse to ashes during cremation is usually about an hour and a half.

During the French Revolution miniature models of the guillotine were made and produced at dinner parties, some with small figures which, when beheaded, proved to be filled with liquor for gentlemen guests or perfume for ladies.

In 1873 a Scottish judge passed a death sentence which erroneously resulted in the prisoner escaping the gallows altogether, for m'lud sentenced him to die 'on Tuesday the 29th April next to come'. Luckily for the condemned man, 29 April would not fall on a Tuesday for the next six years, so his sentence was commuted to imprisonment instead.

A statute passed in Virginia, America, in 1662, declared that 'The court in every county shall cause to be set up near a Court House, a Pillory, a pair of Stocks, a Whipping Post and a Ducking Stool, in such a place as they think convenient; any not set up within six months after the date of this Act, the said Court will be fined 5,000lbs of tobacco.'

Frank Plaia, sentenced to die in the electric chair in 1929, suddenly contracted appendicitis, so surgeons successfully performed the necessary operation; then the authorities electrocuted him.

During execution in the electric chair, the victim's bodily temperature rises to 140°F.

One wouldn't expect a clergyman to be capable of murder, but that was the case when Avis Liddell was found dead in 1911 at Boston's YWCA hostel. Having become engaged to another woman, the Reverend Richeson gave Avis a pill to induce an abortion; in fact it contained cyanide, and so, on 20 May 1912, he found himself escorted, not by the best man up the aisle, but by prison officers to the electric chair.

The New York *Weekly Post Boy* carried an item in 1745 regarding a Dr Attwood 'who is remembered as the first doctor who had the hardihood to proclaim himself a man-midwife; it was deemed scandalous to some delicate ears, and Mrs Granny Brown, with her fees of two or three dollars, was still deemed the choice of all who thought that women should be modest.'

The RAF Church of St Clement Danes in London is so called because it was built on a Danish burial site.

An early American prescription to reduce pain in childbirth was quoted by the son of Governor Endicott in the 1660s: 'For Sharpe & dificult Travel [travail, labour] in Women with child, Take a Lock of Vergins haire on any Part of ye head, of half the Age of ye Woman in travill. Cut it very smale to fine Powder then take twelve Ants Eggs dried in an oven after ye bread is drawne or other wise make them dry & make them to powder with the haire, give this with a quarter of a pint of Red Cows milk or for want of it give it in strong ale wort.'

The poet Ben Jonson was buried in Westminster Abbey in 1572, in an upright position 'so that, come Judgment Day, he would have a head start over the others!'

Potatoes were introduced into Europe in the sixteenth century, not as a food but as an expensive medicine having aphrodisiac properties.

When Abbé Delorme was tried for murder in Canada in 1922, one prosecution exhibit was a tailor's dummy, dressed in the blood-stained garments and cap worn by his brother, the victim of the savage shooting.

A tumbrel was the vehicle used to convey victims to the guillotine.

Patrick Cotter, alias O'Brian, was born in 1761. At the age of 26 he measured 8ft 7ins in height; his hand, from the palm to the tip of his middle finger, measured 12ins and his shoes were 17ins. long. He exercised in the streets early in the mornings and, to light his pipe, took the top off a street gas-lamp. He died in 1807 of consumption, aged 46.

In 1773 a female dwarf was exhibited in London; a native of Corsica, named Madame Teresa or the Corsican Fairy, she was only 2ft 10ins tall and weighed 26lbs.

Drastic earthquakes occurred in England in 1750. Starting with heat waves in the early spring, a shock was felt on 8 February and a month later a more severe one shook London 'in which the bells of the churches struck against the chiming-hammers, dogs howled and fish jumped high out of the water. Houses collapsed, many residents fleeing into the country. Earthquake gowns, warm gowns to wear while sitting out of doors all night, were in great demand by women.'

Even as now, those committing minor offences in the old days were fined. Ancient records show that in 1494 Robert Smith was fined 8d. for refusing to bury a dead pig; on 7 February 1576 Jas. Hartas, 'ote-meall maker, for drying oats upon the Saboth day', paid out 3s. 4d.; on 15 August 1577 Jno. Levytt was fined 4d. for making 'a paire of shoes of unlawfull stuffe', and four other men had to pay 3s. 4d. each for selling candles above the price assigned them by the Mayor.

Had it not been for something resembling a glove found floating in the Murrumbidgee River in Australia, the savage death of Percy Smith would never have been avenged. His body was found in the river on Christmas Day 1933, but it had deteriorated so much that recognition of the cadaver was impossible until the discovery of the 'glove' further along the river bank; this grue-some find turned out to be the skin from one of the corpse's hands, so complete that a detective was able to slide his own hand inside. Fingerprints taken from it led to the identification of the body. Incriminating evidence was found in the possession of a companion, Edward Morey, and justice duly ran its course.

In December 1994 a young American girl student took many photos around London including some of the Tower. When she returned to the States the films were developed and printed, and one of them, taken at Traitors' Gate, showed what appeared to be a hand and an arm clad in what was unmistakably Tudor dress. The negative (now in the possession of the author) was professionally analysed by the film manufacturers, who stated that it was not a double negative, the image had not been com-puter generated and the 'hand' was there when the photograph had been taken and not inserted later. So what was it? And what would have been on the print had the student stood further back?

In an identity parade the victim of a crime usually walks along a line of 'suspects' and points out the person they identify, but the routine was different when Alfred Moore was suspected of shooting a police inspector and constable in 1951. The inspector died shortly afterwards, but at an identity parade held in the hospital ward the dying constable recognised his attacker, and Moore was subsequently hanged.

According to the court records of 1606, Susannah Ritlin of Regenstauff, Germany, 'had a child by a nail-maker. When she gave birth to it secretly, she wrung its little neck, put it in a pot, and threw it down a privy and into the river Pegnitz. Instead of being hanged, she was beheaded as a favour.'

During the World War II German bombing raids on London, Mme Tussaud's Waxworks Museum took a direct hit, and 295 moulds of male heads and 57 moulds of female heads were found smashed in the huge crater. Many of the life-size models were also badly damaged. One can only imagine the reactions of would-be rescuers on seeing the shattered heads and body parts.

Few people facing death on the gallows compose themselves for the ordeal; fewer still compose a song to sing while being noosed, yet Kenneth Neu, a double murderer, stood on the New Orleans scaffold in 1933 warbling his lyrics, the first line of which was 'I'm as fit as a fiddle and ready to hang.'

St Thomas More sometimes tied religious heretics to the 'Tree of Life' in his garden and whipped them.

In 1500 the great Cardinal Wolsey was seen to be drunk at a village feast at Lymington, Yeovil, by Amyas Poulett, the local Justice of the Peace, who sentenced him to be put in the stocks.

After William Lee, a double rapist, had been hanged on Smith's Island, Maryland, in July 1906, there was a hectic scramble for souvenirs; some memorabilia collectors were allowed pieces of the rope, but the fisherman who attempted to cut off and keep one of the felon's ears was prevented from doing so.

Chaplains were forbidden to speak to the condemned man after the noose had been positioned, following a case in 1903 when, just as the hangman was about to release the drop trapdoors, the clergyman stepped forward and asked the felon whether he was guilty or not guilty. The answer was 'Guilty', but the immediate consequences, had he stated the opposite, could well have caused the executioner to pause at that crucial moment and so delay the despatch of the victim.

The monument erected in 1761 in Westminster Abbey to Lady Nightingale included a fearsome marble figure of Death. It was reported that a burglar who broke into the building one night was so terrified on seeing the figure in the moonlight that he promptly fled in terror. The crowbar which he dropped in his haste was left by the tomb for many years for tourists to wonder at.

During the French Revolution, 'to look through the little window' was a colloquialism for being guillotined, because one's head was pinned down by the iron collar or *lunette*.

Reginald Birchall was hanged for the murder of Fred Benwell in 1890 in Canada. On the scaffold, he asked the hangman to shake hands with him, and smiled. It was reported later 'that those who performed the post-mortem found the smile still lingering about his ashen lips.'

Daniel Lambert was born in 1770, a normal sized baby, but by 1793 he weighed 448lbs and by 1805 this had increased to 700lbs. He exhibited himself in London for many years and died on 21 July 1809. His coffin was 6ft 4ins long, 4ft 4ins wide and 2ft 4ins deep; it was made from 112ft of elm and, mounted on two axles having two cogwheels each, was rolled into his grave.

Child protection, fourteenth-century style: the hurers, makers of cheap fur caps and capes, needing to clean the furs by scouring them in water, 'had been sending children of tender age down to the Thames and other exposed places, amid horrible tempests, frosts and snows, to the very great scandal of the City.'

In the seventeenth century, those who sowed sedition (spread treason) were branded with the letter S on each side of the nose.

After the accomplices of American assassin John Wilkes Booth had been hanged, their cadavers were placed in coffins, together with small bottles containing their names.

On the occasion of the last public hanging in Northampton, which took place in 1852, thousands gathered to watch the execution, but at the last moment the authorities changed the day. At that, some of the disappointed spectators declared that 'if they could only get at the Under-sheriff, they would let him know what it was like to keep honest folk in suspense, one old woman even exclaiming that she had a mind to claim expenses from the council!'

A report submitted by an official inspector at the time of the sixteenth-century Dissolution of the Monasteries stated that he, with five others, 'found the Prior of the Crossed Friars in London, at that tyme beying in bedde with his hoore, both nakyd, about xi in the fornune, upon a Friday.'

When Samuel Pepys complained of itching, his wife cut his hair and inspected his shirt, finding no fewer than twenty lice. The renowned diarist exclaimed that they were 'little and great, more than I have had these twenty years'.

John Bennett was charged with murdering his wife Mary Jane in September 1900 and, despite protesting his innocence, was hanged in Norwich Gaol in March of the following year. When the black flag on the prison roof was hoisted, indicating that the execution had taken place, the flagpole snapped; many took this as a sign that Bennett had been falsely accused, but by then he was in no position to agree.

Frederick Browne and William Kennedy brutally murdered Police Constable Gutteridge in 1927; believing that they would be caught because their images would remain on the officer's retinas, Browne fired a shot into each of his eyes. They were both hanged in London in May 1928.

Author and poet Tom May, who died in 1650, was renowned for his roistering and heavy drinking. It was reported that he died because 'on going to bed after a hearty supper, he tied his night-cap too close under his fat cheeks and chin, which choked him when he turned on to his other side.'

Henrietta, Duchess of Marlborough, who inherited £10,000 from the dramatist and poet William Congreve after his death in 1729, had an ivory statuette of him, operated by clockwork, positioned on the dinner table, and not only had dishes set before it but carried on conversations as if it were William himself. She also had a wax image made of him, the feet of which she daily blistered, in memory of the agonies he had suffered from gout.

In 1786 a gentleman of antiquarian tastes received permission to enter a tomb in Westminster Abbey in which lay the coffins of the Duke of Cumberland and others, in order to copy the inscription on the ducal coffin. Unfortunately his presence there was over-looked by those responsible for locking the Abbey doors, 'the man having to remain among the tombs until released the next morning, more dead than alive with sheer terror.'

A medical advertisement in London's *Morning Chronicle* in 1766 was placed by Mr Patence, 'a dentist, dancing master and quack', in which he claimed that his Supreme Pills would cure palsies, gout, rheumatism, piles, fistulas, cancers of any sort, King's Evil, infections, jaundice, green sickness, convulsions, scorbutic diseases and pains in the head, brain, temple, arteries, face, nose, mouth and limbs. The Pills also restored hearing and sight, renewed the vital and animal vitalities, gave complexion to the face, 'and many times has given unexpected relief on the verge of eternity.' Price, 3s.; with personal advice, 10s. 6d.

During the siege of Londonderry in the seventeenth century food ran so short for the defenders that they had to eat whatever animals were available; the price of a small dog was 2s. a quarter and horse blood 4d. a pint.

In the West Indies, when settlers employed slaves to work long hours in appalling conditions on their plantations, beatings were frequent. If death resulted, it was not a hanging matter; the plantation owner simply paid the value of the slave as a fine.

A German visitor to England in 1782 wrote: 'Nothing in London makes so disgusting an appearance to a foreigner as the butchers' shops, especially in the environs of the Tower; guts and all the nastiness are thrown into the middle of the street and cause an unsupportable stench.'

Totally unconcerned when found guilty of kidnapping and murdering Charles Ross in Chicago in 1937, and then killing his own accomplice James Gray, Henry Seadland casually asked, 'Will I be hanged or fried?' The noose having been abandoned by the state, he later took his place in the electric chair.

The American state of Georgia was founded in the early 1700s by General James Edward Oglethorpe. He died in 1785 and, when the state authorities requested that his body be buried there, permission was refused, on the grounds that an Englishman should be buried in his own country wherever possible.

In days of yore it was not unusual for women to fight each other for prizes. To prevent them using their 'natural' weapons, their finger nails, they had to clutch a coin in each hand during the bout; should one drop a coin, they would be declared the loser. In June 1768 two women fought each other in Spa-fields, Islington, 'Bruising Peg' winning the prize, a new chemise.

The *Universal Magazine* of February 1775 related how, when a Mr Brower, en route to Enfield, was attacked by a robber, he recognised the man as a tradesman in the City and called him by his name; his assailant promptly shot himself through the head.

In 1790 Renwick Williams was imprisoned for six years, having been caught stabbing women 'in a part of their bodies that gallantry and manhood considered sacred'.

During the first crossing of the Channel by Jean-Pierre Blanchard and Dr Jeffries in a hydrogen-filled balloon in 1785, they started to lose height and jettisoned all moveable items. This proved insufficient, but, as the Doctor later related, 'we had drunk much at breakfast and had not had any evacuation; because of the severe cold we had not perspired, and so we decided to discharge the contents of our kidneys. Using two bladders from the balloon we were able to obtain between five and six pounds of urine which, when dropped over the side, helped us to maintain a safe altitude until landing.' It is hoped that they first warned the spectators not to look up!

In 1900 the plague began to ravage San Francisco. Although more than a million rats were destroyed in the city in an attempt to limit the spread of the disease, it infected ground squirrels in the neighbouring countryside and twenty million of them had to be slaughtered. This proved effective, for only two hundred plague deaths were reported among the populace.

When the death of Colonel Blood, the would-be thief of the Crown Jewels, was announced, suspicions arose that it was a ruse and that the cunning colonel would appear later and get up to new tricks. Accordingly the corpse was exhumed and its identity confirmed by examining the thumb of the left hand, which was known to be twice the usual size.

In 1584 Jerome Beyhlstein of Nuremberg encouraged his wife to become a prostitute; he would then send a bill to each of the men who had availed themselves of her services. For that crime he was whipped out of town. His wife was executed.

Dr Bougrat hid Jacques Rumebe's dead body in a cupboard in his surgery – after stealing the twenty thousand francs his friend had had with him – and carefully papered over its doors. Unfortunately, while a body can be concealed, the smell of slowly decomposing flesh cannot. Neighbours complained, excuses such as dead mice under the floor boards were rejected and Bougrat was arrested. Despite claiming that Rumebe had committed suicide by injecting himself with arsenic while alone in the surgery, and that he had hidden the corpse through panic, in 1927 Bougrat was sentenced to life imprisonment on Devil's Island.

But, incredibly, he managed to escape to Venezuela, where, as a doctor, he was permitted to remain until his death 35 years later.

Mme Tussaud started her sculpting career by making death masks of those guillotined during the French Revolution.

So great was the mortality rate from yellow fever among the French who were endeavouring to build the Panama Canal in the 1880s that it was said that there was a Frenchman buried under every tie of the Panama Railway.

In days long gone, tobacco users were deterred by threats far worse than the risk of contracting lung disease. In 1624 the Pope warned snuff takers that he would excommunicate them; the Turkish Government brought in the death sentence for smokers; and the Russian Emperor declared that 'tobacco drinkers' would have their noses slit and be thoroughly whipped, then sent into exile in Siberia.

Samuel Pepys described Nell Gwynne, Charles II's mistress, as having the smallest feet of any woman in England. She was illiterate and, before dying of apoplexy in her 38th year in 1687, signed her will 'EG' (Eleanor Gwynne).

When hanged, felons' bodies gyrated slowly on the rope, which led to a comment by the American murderer John McDonald, who, when a spectator said he had seen him before, exclaimed: 'Yes, and if you wait until Jack Ketch has done with me, I'll turn round so's you can see me behind!'

When Sir Henry Royce of Rolls-Royce fame died in 1933, his will contained a clause expressing his wish that he should be cremated and his ashes buried beneath the floor of his first workshop in Derby.

A colony of English settlers in Virginia in 1622 was visited by local Red Indians who brought gifts of deer, turkeys, fish and fruit. The following day 'they came freely and seemingly unarmed till they fell to work all at once everywhere, knocking the English on the head with tomahawks and axes, sparing neither age nor sex.'

During the French Revolution the tombs in La Tombe Isoire cemetery were sold and desecrated, the ground cleared and a dance hall, named the 'Hall of Victims', built on the site. Only those whose relatives had been guillotined were admitted, the women wearing their hair up, as if ready to be beheaded; their slogan was 'We dance among the Tombs'.

In order to reduce the number of mad dogs running wild in the City of London in 1760 the Lord Mayor offered a bounty of half-a-crown (12½p) for every dog's head that was brought to the Mansion House, 'but after paying out 438 half-crowns, he began to sicken of his zeal, which he found too expensive.'

In her will, Frances Stuart, Duchess of Lennox, who died on 15 October 1702, stated that a wax effigy of her should be made, 'dressed in my Coronation Robes and Coronett', and that her pet parrot, which had lived with her for upwards of forty years, should, upon its death, be displayed with her effigy. And so it was, duly stuffed.

Following the 1915 murder of Margaret Wolcott in Orleans County, New York, Charles Stielow was tried and sentenced to death. Many temporary appeals were granted and ultimately he was found not guilty – but it was a near thing, for the reprieve arrived while he was actually strapped in the electric chair.

When the Earl of Strafford, known as 'Black Tom Tyrant' for his harsh methods of quelling the Irish, was executed, the thousands of spectators afterwards ran through the streets shouting 'His head is off! His head is off!' and smashed the windows of those who failed to celebrate with them by lighting bonfires.

During the reign of Charles II, so beautiful was Francis Theresa Stuart that she was used as the model of Britannia on the reverse of penny and halfpenny coins. In her will she left directions that her body should not be opened, but 'should be packed in bran before it is cold, and buried wrapped in the sheets wherein my Lord [her husband Charles, Duke of Lennox] and I first slept that night we were married.'

Nearly a dozen people, men, women and children, were murdered by Peter Manuel in Scotland in the mid-1950s, and on 11 July 1958 he was hanged in Barlinnie Gaol, Glasgow. While researching this book, the author stood on the very drop trapdoors on which Manuel had stood – a decidedly macabre sensation.

Werner Boost, the 'Doubles Killer', operated in Düsseldorf in the 1950s, creeping up to the parked cars of courting couples and shooting them dead. He even toyed with the outlandish idea of murdering his prey by filling balloons with liquid cyanide and releasing them in the vehicles. Caught by an observant forest ranger, he was found guilty and in 1959 was sentenced to life imprisonment.

According to the inscription on his tomb in Westminster Abbey, 'Old Parr' lived through the reigns of ten sovereigns: Edward IV, Edward V, Richard III, Henry VII, Henry VIII, Edward VI, Mary, Elizabeth I, James I and Charles I. He was born in 1483 and died in 1635, having lived for 152 years 9 months. He married when he was 80, and at the age of 105 paid penance in church 'for unchaste behaviour with a Katherine Milton'! His wife died when he was 112, and he married again ten years later.

A tax of 6s. 8d. (33p) was levied on every pound of tobacco in 1604. Its purpose was to deter those 'who, through evil custom, is taken by disordered persons of base condition, that they consume their wages, impair their health and weaken their bodies, and are driven thereby to unthrifty shifts to maintain their gluttonous habits.'

Young lovers in the new colony of America ran dire risks, as evidenced by a Plymouth law dated 1638: 'Whereas divers persons unfit for marriage both in regard of their young yeares, as also in their weake estate [lack of money] are practiseing the inveagling of men's daughters, and maids with gardians, contrary to their parents and gardians likeings [wishes], and of maide servants without the leave and likeing of their masters; it is therefore enacted by the Court that if any shall make a motion of marriage to any man's daughter or mayde-servant, not having first obtayned leave and consent of the parents or master, soe to doe, shall be punished either by fine or corporall punishment, or both, at the discretions of the Bench and according to the nature of the offense.'

Elizabethan etiquette in 1577 advised: 'Blow not your nose on the napkin, but cleanse it in your handkerchief; and if thou must spit or blow thy nose, keep thou it out of sight; let it not lie upon the ground, but tread thou it outright.'

'Running footmen' were servants who accompanied the carriages of the rich in the eighteenth century, both as escorts and also to assist their employers to alight on reaching their destination. To give them the stamina required to keep up with the horse-drawn vehicles, they carried hollow white canes containing a mixture of egg and wine.

The Duchess of Northumberland asked for her funeral in Westminster Abbey to be private, but the ceremony that took place in December 1776 was far from that. So great was the crowd that one tomb, on the top of which men and boys had perched, was brought crashing down; the funeral was delayed for two hours, and finally took place while those who had been injured were still crying for help.

When a statue of engineer James Watt was being moved into Westminster Abbey soon after his death in 1819, its weight was so great that a crack opened up in the Abbey's floor and 'disclosed to the eyes of the astonished workmen, rows upon rows of gilded coffins in the vaults beneath, into which, but for the planking placed earlier, they would have descended, thereby joining the dead in the chamber of death.'

In a letter to a friend dated 19 November 1834, Sydney Smith wrote: 'I am better in health, avoiding all fermented liquors, and drinking nothing but London water, with a million insects in every drop. He who drinks a tumblerful of London water has literally in his stomach more animated beings than there are men, women and children on the face of the globe!'

Murderer John George Haigh blithely imagined that without a body, there could be no murder trial, so he murdered Olive Durand-Deacon for her money and dumped her body in a vat of sulphuric acid he had prepared, after removing her fur coat and jewellery. Assuming that her body would dissolve, he was confident of being found innocent, even when arrested with the jewellery in his possession; but it was not to be, and he was hanged on 10 August 1949, doubtless kicking himself for not removing Olive's dentures as well – because they didn't melt away.

The historian Erasmus (1466–1536) described how in English houses 'the floors are covered with rushes, occasionally removed,

but so imperfectly that the bottom layer is left undisturbed, sometimes for twenty years, harbouring expectorations, vomiting,
leakages of dogs and man, all droppings, scraps of fish and other
abominations not fit to be mentioned.' He also added some tips
on behaviour when in company, writing: 'It is very rude to blow
your nose on the table cloth or wipe your fingers on your neighbour's coat. Above all, do not lick your plate; it is an act that
ill-becomes a cat, let alone a gentleman!'

Transporting precious stones in the wilder parts of the world in
the sixteenth century always posed problems, as the French
Ambassador, M. Nicholas Harlei, found out when sending a diamond, the Great Sanci, to the King of France. Some time after his
trusted servant had left, news came that he had been waylaid and
probably robbed and killed. Having ridden to the forest where
the attack occurred, Harlei searched and eventually found the
messenger's grave. Never doubting the man's loyalty and quick
thinking ability, he had his men exhume the corpse; then, without hesitation, ordered them to open the stomach. As he had
suspected, his faithful servant, on being attacked, had thwarted
the thieves by swallowing the gem.

During the French Revolution the guillotine became part of
Parisian life. Some citizens even delighted in beheading the stone
statues that adorned churches. Those in the porches of the old
basilica of Notre-Dame all lost their heads; the whiteness of the
broken stone, contrasting with the figure that was blackened by
time, gave an impression of freshly-cut flesh.

Not every subject of Henry VI appreciated his sense of humour,
but three men were thankful for it, once they had got over
their initial shock. Accused of high treason in 1447, they were
sentenced to be hanged, drawn and quartered. On the scaffold
they were duly suspended from the gallows for the requisite

short length of time, after which they were cut down, half-strangled. The executioner proceeded to mark their bodies for the quartering process – then the sheriff stepped forward and informed them that they had been pardoned.

Stephen Bradley kidnapped eight-year-old Graeme Thorne in Sydney, Australia, on 7 July 1960 and, although demanding a ransom, killed the boy. He was caught when plant particles found on the body were identified as those of two species of cypress trees; eventually the police found a house in the garden of which, unusually, both species grew together. The house had been occupied by Bradley, who had fled following the failure of the ransom demand. Arrested and found guilty, he received a sentence of life imprisonment, which gave him plenty of time to study dendrology.

The renowned poet John Donne once had a full-sized sketch drawn of himself, eyes closed, wearing a shroud. It was later used to sculpt a monument to him in St Paul's Cathedral after his death in 1572.

The Times for 13 July 1948 reported that 'Mr Joe Simms aged 51, a Southampton dock worker, yesterday crossed the Thames at Chelsea by what he claims to be a new method of progress through water. It took him seventeen minutes to "walk" across the river with only his head showing above the water, his arms folded across his chest, and his hands on his shoulders. The whole time he was in the water he appeared to be perfectly erect and twice waved his arms to the crowds on the banks and on the bridge, and doffed the cap which he wore and waved it. Mr Simms said afterwards that his movement was made with a slow cycle action. He described it as a triumph of mind over matter, and the coordination of mind and limbs. "I can kneel on salt water and can recline with my head resting on my arms," he added.'

The word 'buccaneer' originated with the pirates who first settled in Haiti, many of whom were French, the word being derived from their staple diet, meat that had been *boucaned*, or dried. Long strips of both beef and pork, the latter from wild hogs, were salted and dried in ovens until they were brown and as hard as cardboard, but even after being stored for a year, when soaked in lukewarm water, they became 'plump and rosy enough to entice the most languid appetite'. A similar delicacy is the 'biltong' of South Africa.

The funeral of Sir Bernard Turner, Sheriff of London in the 1780s, was far from dignified and the burial far from punctual, because a legal attempt had been made to arrest the corpse for debt, and it was not until the creditors had been paid that the cortège was allowed to proceed.

There is nothing new under the sun. Graffiti were widespread in the eighteenth century, even respectable travellers writing their names on the windows of the inns in which they lodged; lacking diamond rings, some of them carried diamond pencils for that purpose.

A cock-fight enthusiast three centuries ago needed to have a head for heights. If he lost a bet and was unable to pay up, he would be put into a basket and hoisted to the ceiling, there to remain until the end of the bouts.

Some members of the public were always suspicious that free-masons showed favouritism towards fellow brothers, but this was far from the truth when Frederick Seddon was being tried for murder in 1912. Both the accused and the judge were free-masons, and when Seddon indicated as much, the judge replied in an emotional voice, 'Our brotherhood does not encourage crime, it condemns it. Make your peace with the Great Architect of the

Universe. Mercy – pray for it; ask for it.' He then sentenced
Seddon to death.

Anyone who fondly believes that people living in the nineteenth
century were prim and proper needs to think again after reading
this account by a foreigner visiting England in 1810. Describing
the manners of the English at the table, he wrote: 'Drinking much
and long leads to unavoidable consequences. Will it be credited
that, in a corner of the very dining room, there is a certain convenient piece of furniture, to be used by anybody who wants it.
The operation is performed very deliberately and undisguised, as
a matter of course, and occasions no interruption of the conversation. I once took the liberty of asking why this convenient
article was not placed out of the room and was told that otherwise, men of weak heads or stomacks would take advantage of
the opportunity to make their escape shamefully, before they
were quite drunk!'

Old London Bridge was built by Peter de Colechurch in 1176,
and when he died in 1205 his body was entombed in the chapel
of the church which, together with many houses and shops, had
been constructed on the bridge. It was not until 1832, when the
old bridge was being demolished and a new one built, that his
remains were discovered, having lain there for over six hundred
years.

Alphonse Bertillon, a Paris police officer, introduced a method of
identifying criminals in 1880 based on the assumption that no
two people had the same combination of certain measurements,
such as the width of the head, the length of the face, of the ear,
the middle finger, the limbs from knee to foot, etc. This procedure was time-consuming and error-prone, and was replaced by
1900, when individual differences between finger-prints were
discovered.

It is believed that the length of a yard, three feet, was decided upon by Henry I, who declared it to be the distance from the tip of the regal nose to the tip of the royal thumb on the King's outstretched arm.

Accused of three murders in 1982, Canadian Clifford Olson promptly offered to show the police where he'd killed and buried eight more – but only at a price of $10,000 each, making $110,000 for the lot. The authorities accepted his offer but reduced it to $90,000, placing it in a trust fund for Olson's son, and sentencing the killer to a life sentence for each murder as well.

American Carl Panzram, on the Fort Leavenworth scaffold in 1929, urged the hangman to hurry up. 'I could hang a dozen men while you're fooling around!' the murderer exclaimed angrily.

Charles Guiteau, who murdered US President James Garfield in July 1881, left a letter stating that any person who desired to honour his remains could do so by erecting a monument whereon should be inscribed these words: 'Here lies the body of Charles Guiteau, Patriot and Christian; his soul is in glory.'

M. De Sartines, a French Minister of Police in the eighteenth century, had a novel way of entertaining distinguished guests at his many parties: he would order some of 'his' thieves, who were adroit pickpockets, to attend and perform their tricks: cutting his guests' watch chains, and stealing their purses, snuff boxes and items of jewellery.

The notorious pirate Captain Kidd was probably unaware of being launched into eternity, for he was drunk when the noose was placed around his neck.

Hot dogs are a popular food, but surely not when they are real dogs! Nevertheless, 'eat more dogs' was a slogan in Cambodia in 2003, endorsed by the authorities, to reduce the number of canines roaming the cities. The governor of the capital, Phnom Penh, urged everyone to chew a chow, saying, 'Come on, dog meat is so delicious!'

In October 1552 two 'monsters of the whale kind' were sighted in the Thames and, after being chased for two days and nights, were killed at Woolwich. As it was thought that the king would be interested to see them, they were towed by barges under London Bridge to Whitehall, where they were later displayed to Edward VI.

Certain South American Indians, lacking needles and surgical thread, developed an ingenious method of stitching wounds. Pressing the edges of the wound together, they held it over leaf-cutter ants; when an ant closed its powerful jaws on the wound, they would cut its body off and leave the jaws in place until the wound had healed.

Peter Kürten was known as the 'Monster of Düsseldorf', a title well earned: sexually stimulated by the sight of blood, he slew at least nine men, women and even animals, as well as committing countless other violent crimes. On mounting the guillotine scaffold in 1931 he expressed his regret, not for his crimes, but because he would not be able to hear his own blood pumping out after the blade had fallen.

John of Gaddesden, born in 1280, became physician to Edward II and proceeded to make his fortune by always prescribing twice as much medicine for his rich clients as he did for his poorer ones, whether they needed it or not, and charging them accordingly. He was also probably the first doctor to realise the potential of cosmetic treatments, and sold prescriptions for perfumes, shampoos, hair dye and similar appearance-improvers, thereby originating today's multi-million-pound industry.

In 2003 it was reported that a passenger in a Chinese airliner attempted to commit hara-kiri by slitting his stomach open with a pair of scissors; he was eventually subdued with tranquillisers after smashing his head against the side of the plane, and was arrested on arrival in Beijing.

A fourteenth-century method of ascertaining whether a patient was dead or not was 'to apply lightly roasted onion to his nostrils; if he be alive, he will immediately scratch his nose.'

Curators of the Hermitage Museum in St Petersburg removed an icon of Christ in 2003 after complaints that a 'negative energy biofield' emanating from it seriously affected the health of people sitting near it, by making their brains vibrate at a high frequency.

Manned balloons caused much excitement before the advent of aeroplanes, but the one that drew immense crowds on Queen Victoria's coronation day regrettably ended with a fatality. The craft took to the air from Hyde Park, piloted by Captain Curie, with a Mrs Graham as passenger. The balloon ascended only a few feet and, as there was no wind, just hovered there. The gallant captain endeavoured to gain altitude by releasing some ballast, steadfastly ignoring facetious suggestions from the spectators that he should throw out Mrs Graham as well! After a while the balloon floated away, to come to earth again in Marylebone; as it did so, although the two on board escaped injury, the basket dislodged some stonework, killing a passer-by.

When any well-known personage was condemned to death, his execution at Tyburn was a great event, especially for the entrepreneurs who erected stands around the scaffold and charged exorbitant prices for the seats; but financial disaster overtook them in 1758 when a last-minute reprieve arrived for the traitor Dr Henesey and the crowd, thwarted of its entertainment, proceeded to destroy the entire structure.

For centuries the task of helping women in labour was that of midwives and never doctors; a woman's body was sacrosanct and should never be intimately revealed to members of the male sex. Physicians, however believed they could save many lives if they were in attendance. Dr Wertt of Hamburg, knowing he would not under any circumstances be admitted to the lying-in room, yet realising that that was the only way he could study the process of birth, dressed as a woman and visited the next confinement in his district. Initially all went well, but his masquerade was discovered, and in 1522 he was burned at the stake.

Aleister Crowley, who died in 1947, boasted that he was the wickedest man in the world and claimed the title of the 'Great Beast'. He devoted himself to Satanism and was leader of a cult which indulged in witchcraft and extreme sexual orgies. His behaviour was so degenerate that not only did both his wives end their days in institutions for the insane, but five of his many mistresses committed suicide.

To satisfy the industrial demand for iron during World War II, railings around parks and houses were removed by the authorities; those around Buckingham Place yielded twenty tons of the much-wanted metal.

Living in seventeenth-century houses must have strained the eyesight more than somewhat, especially when the government introduced the Window Tax, all residences with more than seven windows being charged accordingly. Many householders promptly bricked up the eighth and other windows, creating a Stygian gloom indoors that was hardly dispelled by the candles and flickering oil lamps of the day.

Martin Van Butchell was a quack dentist who rode up and down Rotten Row, London, on a white pony painted with purple spots. When his wife died in January 1775 he had her body embalmed and, to make her look more presentable, fitted her with two glass eyes and reddened her cheeks and lips with an injection of a carmine solution. He then dressed this improved version of his missus in linen and lace and, placing her in a glass case in his sitting-room, formally introduced her to visitors as his 'dear departed'.

Refuse collection was unknown in London in the 1700s, and filth and ordure piled up in huge heaps. A rubbish tip at the end of Gray's Inn Lane, however, was put to an unusual use: shipped to Russia, it was made into bricks with which to rebuild Moscow.

Surgeon Astley Cooper, born in 1768, practised his dissection skills on dead animals acquired from the Tower Zoo. On one occasion an elephant died; the size of the crowd watching the animal's corpse being transported from the Tower can well be imagined, and so, as the beast was too large for the dissecting room, the surgeon and his pupils had to dissect it in the courtyard, concealing operations from the general public by draping carpets over the railings.

Ted Williams killed his three young daughters in 1924 in order, he said, to spare them the hardships of life, and was sentenced to death by the Sydney courts. The New South Wales Minister of Justice, Thomas Ley, rejected an appeal for clemency and Williams was hanged. Curiously, 23 years later, in 1947, Ley himself was sentenced to death for murder in England but, being declared insane, was committed to Broadmoor Lunatic Asylum, where he later died.

After experimenting with cathode rays in November 1895, Professor Wilhelm Conrad Roentgen of Würzburg reported a phenomenon he had discovered: rays that would mysteriously penetrate articles such as books, clothing and even human flesh. Not knowing what to call them, he referred to them as 'X-rays'. To the world's media the ability of X-rays to see through solid objects was headline news, and such was its impact that a London firm made a fortune selling ladies X-ray-proof under-wear. But spoil-sport morality groups in the United States petitioned Congress to issue laws forbidding the use of X-rays in opera glasses in the theatre.

One wonders whether Mr Green shouted 'Up, up and away!' or 'Gee up!' when, in 1850, he made a balloon ascent while astride a horse which had been secured to the gasbag. The SPCA protested in vain.

A will not to be sniffed at! One such, made out on 2 April 1776, said: 'In the Name of God, Amen. I, Margaret Thompson, being of sound mind, etc. do desire that when my soul is departed from this wicked world, my body and effects may be disposed of in the manner following. I desire that all my handkerchiefs that I may have unwashed at the time of my decease, after they have been gotten together by my old and trusty servant Sarah Stuart, to be put by her, and by her alone, at the bottom of my coffin, which I desire may be made big enough for that purpose, together with such a quantity of the best Scotch snuff, in which she knoweth I always had the greatest delight, as will cover my deceased body; and this I desire the more especially as it is usual to put flowers into the coffins of departed friends, and nothing can be so fragrant and refreshing to me as that precious powder. But I strictly charge that no man be suffered to approach my body till the coffin is closed, and it is necessary to carry me to my burial, which I order in the manner following; Six men to be my bearers, who are known to be the greatest snuff-takers in the parish of St James, Westminster; instead of mourning headgear, each to wear a snuff-coloured beaver hat, which I desire may be bought for that purpose, and given to them. Six maidens of my old acquaintance are to bear my pall, each to wear a proper hood and to carry a box filled with the best Scotch snuff to take for their refreshment as they go along. Before my corpse, I desire the minister may be invited to walk and to take a certain quantity of the said snuff, not exceeding one pound, to whom also I bequeath five guineas on condition of his doing so. And I also desire my old and faithful servant, Sarah Stuart, to walk before the corpse and distribute every twenty yards, a large handful of Scotch snuff to the ground and upon the crowd who may possibly follow me to the burial place; on which condition I bequeath her 20s. And I also desire that at least two bushels of the said snuff may be distributed to others at the door of my house in Boyle Street.' That should make the Day of Judgment a lively, if noisy, affair!

London's Mayfair was originally, of course, the site of the annual May-Fair, attracting hundreds of entertainers and thousands of Londoners. Among those who put on shows for the public was, as described by a visitor from out of town, 'a Frenchman who demonstrated to the curious, the astonishing strength of the Strong Woman, his wife. A blacksmith's anvil having been procured from White Horse street, with three of the men, they brought it in and placed it on the floor. The woman was short, but most beautifully and delicately formed, and of a lovely countenance. She first let down her hair, a light auburn, of a length descending to her knees, which she twisted round the projecting part of the anvil, and then, with seeming ease, lifted the ponderous weight some inches from the floor. After this, a bed was laid in the middle of the room; when, reclining on her back and uncovering her bosom, the husband ordered the smiths to place thereon the anvil, and forge on it, a horse-shoe! This they obeyed, by taking from the fire a red-hot piece of iron, and with their forging hammers completed the shoe, with the same might and indifference as when in the shop at their usual labours. The prostrate fair one appeared to endure this with the utmost composure, talking and singing during the whole process; then with an effort which seemed, to the by-standers, like some supernatural trial, cast the anvil from her body, jumping up at the same moment with extreme gaiety, and without the least discomposure of her dress or person.'

In the eighteenth century some of those contracting hydrophobia, which was then incurable, were put out of their suffering by being smothered by their friends; under those circumstances, the act was not considered a crime.

Cleopatra's Needle, encased in a cylinder, was shipped from Egypt to England, on board a vessel named after that queen, early in the nineteenth century, but was abandoned in a storm in the Bay of Biscay. Recovered and erected on the Victoria Embankment in 1878, it bears an inscription to the six sailors who lost their lives trying to help the *Cleopatra*'s crew.

Although he was charged in 1960 with thirty-five cases of assault and burglary, twenty cases of rape and ten murders with rape, all that Hans Pommerenke, the 'Beast of the Black Forest', received was a lengthy prison sentence.

It was reported that 'on a single night in 1665 four thousand people were reported to have perished of the Plague in London. A madness seized the inhabitants; distraught with terror they tore off their garments and rushed up and down the streets howling that "the last day had come". One woman was seen rushing down Leadenhall Street with a babe in her arms; on a sudden she perceived the pest spot on its little breast. Crazed with fear, she tore it from her bosom, dashed its brains out on the stones, and sped shrieking along. At the bottom of the street she, too, fell dead, and, the death cart coming along just then, her body, still warm, was borne to Aldgate Churchyard, to join the heaps of corpses already occupying the pit which had been dug there, it being 40ft. long by 16ft. wide and 50ft. deep.'

During World War II Dr Marcel Petiot promised French Jews that for large sums of money he could aid their escape from the Gestapo; he then murdered at least 67 of them and burned their corpses at his Paris home. Despite pleading that his victims had been German soldiers, he was found guilty on at least 24 charges of murder and was guillotined in May 1946.

The corpse of the celebrated Dr John Hunter was interred in St Martin-in-the-Fields church crypt in 1793, but in 1859 a well-known naturalist, Francis Buckland, thought him worthy of a better resting place, namely, Westminster Abbey. He laboriously checked the 2,266 coffins in the crypt and after sixteen days' searching found the one he wanted – coffin number 2,264.

For ten years the body of the 'Pyjama Girl', found brutally murdered, clad only in pyjamas, near Albury in New South Wales in September 1934, was kept in a tank of formalin in Sydney University, pending identification. Some of those questioned thought she might be a Linda Agostini, wife of an immigrant, Antonio Agostini, but he denied knowing the dead woman. In 1944 the case was re-opened; the body was taken out of the bath, washed and dried, her hair combed and make-up applied to her face, and photographs were taken and distributed to the press. Witnesses came forward to confirm her identity and, when confronted by the police, Antonio admitted his guilt. After a prison sentence he was deported to Italy as an undesirable alien.

In 1845 a champion boxer named Caunt fought his challenger, Bendigo of Nottingham, over 88 rounds, which lasted 2 hours 38 minutes. Bendigo won.

It is a curious anomaly that it was Henry VIII's suppression of the monasteries, the hospitals of which provided medical care for all in the locality, that led to the creation of parish registers, in which all baptisms and marriages have been recorded for more than five hundred years.

During the French Revolution, spectators around the scaffold bought brooches shaped like the guillotine. Little has changed since then, for, two hundred years later, in January 1989, when serial killer Robert Bundy was electrocuted in America, entrepreneurs among the crowd outside the jail sold lapel pins in the shape of the electric chair.

Begging was a lucrative way of life in the eighteenth century, especially if the 'beggar' was, or had, an object of pity which might soften the hearts of passers-by. But the risks were great, and the woman who lured children from their parents and then blinded them for that specific purpose was severely whipped by the public hangman from Fleet Street to Temple Bar, much to the satisfaction of the watching public.

Edgar Edwards was found guilty in 1903 of murdering a couple and their ten-week-old child, then dismembering their corpses, in order to take over their property. At the Old Bailey he listened to the judge sentence him to be hanged and exclaimed laughingly, 'Let 'em get along with it as quick as they like!'; on the scaffold he remarked, 'I've been looking forward to this lot!'

A Paris train was wrecked in 1842 when an axle on the leading locomotive broke. Fire raged and, because, in accordance with the rules, the doors had to be locked whenever a train was in motion, 53 passengers were killed. As a result the British Board of Trade immediately ordered the Great Western Railway to stop locking its carriages.

People were just as cynical about public morality in the eighteenth century as they are today. Jonathan Swift wrote that 'An old gentlewoman died here two months ago, and left in her will to have eight men and eight maids as coffin bearers, who should have two guineas (£2 2s.) a-piece, ten guineas to the parson for a sermon, and two guineas to the clerk. But bearers, parson and clerk must all be true virgins, and not be admitted till they took their oaths of virginity; so the poor woman lies still unburied, and must do so till Resurrection Day!'

In the 1800s, London 'sewer-hunters' made a living scavenging below street level for coins and similar valuables accidentally dropped down drains, toilets, etc. Those new to the practice often got lost themselves in the labyrinthine maze of tunnels and, their lamps extinguished by the foul gases, collapsed and died. One sewer-hunter related how 'when I'd got near the grating below the street I'd search about in the bottom of the sewer: I'd put my arm to my shoulder down in the mud and bring up shillings and half-crowns (2s. 6d. pieces), and lots of coppers, and plenty of other things. I once found a silver jug as big as a quart pot, and often found forks and spoons and knives, and everything you can think of. Bless your heart, the smell's nothink; it's a roughish smell at first, but there's lots of water coming down the sewer and the air gets in from the gratings and that helps to sweeten it a bit. Mind you, I've often seen as many as a hundred rats down there at once, and they're woppers in the sewers, I can tell you; them there water rats, too, is far more ferociouser than any other rats

163

and they'd think nothing of tackling a man if they couldn't get away no how, but they runs by and gets out of the road. D'you recollect hearing on the man as was found in the sewers about twelve years ago – oh, you must; the rats ate every bit of him, and left nothink but his bones. I knowed him well, he was a regular down there.'

Sixteenth-century Venetians went to great lengths to keep secret their art of glass-blowing and glass colouring; it was a crime to teach any foreigner how it was done, and soon after one Venetian family had set up a glass factory in Rouen, France, the father, mother, two grown-up sons, a daughter, her husband and their two small children were found stabbed through the heart. On each body was found a paper inscribed *traditore*: traitor.

One most undesirable import from America, which has been with us ever since, arrived during Elizabeth I's reign in cargoes of mahogany: – *cimex lectularius*, the bedbug.

Dr Buck Ruxton, a GP in Lancaster, murdered his wife and maid in 1935 and deposited their dismembered body parts in a Scottish ravine. He was subsequently hanged for their murders. Among the remains was found a 'Cyclops eye' (Cyclops was a mythical giant with one eye in the centre of his forehead, and Cyclopia is a rare malformation in which both eyes are fused together and appear as one). No explanation was forthcoming regarding this bizarre find, although colleagues reported that Dr Ruxton had studied ophthalmology and the 'eye' could have been one of his specimens, which perhaps adhered to one or other of the body parts during the dismembering.

On 9 August 1643 over four thousand women from all over England – among them thirty or forty men wearing petticoats! – surrounded Parliament and presented a petition demanding that

Charles I should rule, not Cromwell. In the fighting that followed, some women and guards were killed; eventually the protesters dispersed and many, finding the call of the local taverns irresistible, finished up drunk in the gutter.

American President George Washington sent the following letter to a ship's captain: 'With this letter comes a negro, Tom, which I beg the favour of you to sell in any of the islands you may go to, for whatever he will fetch, and bring me in return for him, one hhd. [hogshead] of best molasses, one ditto of best rum, one barrel of limes if good and cheap, one pot tamarinds, two small ditto of mixed sweetmeats about 5lb. each, and the residue in good old spirits.'

Individual graves in the eighteenth century existed only for those whose nearest and dearest could pay for the privilege; in the graveyards of such London churches as St-Martin-in-the-Fields and St Giles, the cadavers of paupers were deposited, none too gently, in 'poor holes', deep communal pits dug in the ground, which not were covered with earth until full.

For those who desired really bright and sparkling teeth in 1764, a newspaper advertisement recommended scouring the teeth thoroughly with the end of a meat skewer dipped in gunpowder – though no doubt, if one wanted the washbowl to remain in one piece, it was better not to spit out too violently!

When Joan Cromwell, wife of Oliver Cromwell, moved into the palaces of Whitehall and Hampton Court after the Civil War, she found much opposition from the servants, who had been more accustomed to serving royalty, and she is said to have caused a number of secret passages and trap doors to be constructed 'so as to be able to pounce on them at all times and keep them honest'.

Children have toys to amuse them; royalty had jesters, giants and
dwarfs. The most notable of the latter two categories were
'owned' by Charles I (1625–1649). The smaller gentleman was
Jeffrey Hudson; 18ins tall at the age of seven; 'wholly propor-
tional and without any deformity', he eventually attained a height
of 45ins and once emerged from beneath the pastry lid of a large
pie at a royal banquet. The larger gentleman was William Evans,
6ft 4ins tall; to amaze visiting foreign royalty he would produce
Jeffrey from his pocket. Alas, not everyone appreciated the court
favourites. Little Jeffrey tolerated the taunts for as long as he
could but eventually blew his top – which was very near the
ground, anyway! – and, when a courtier, William Croft, sprayed
him with a water pistol, drew a real pistol and sprayed him with
bullets. Croft died and Jeffrey lost his job.

The current obsession with recycling isn't new. Before being mod-
ernised, a street lamp in Carting Lane, near the Strand, was one
of 'Webb's Patent Sewer Ventilating Lamps', of which thousands
were installed by the Victorians; for fuel they used the malodor-
ous gases from the sewers below ground.

To reduce the effects of drinking an excessive amount of wine, the
Romans would consume quantities of lettuce. The vegetable was
also renowned for its aphrodisiac properties. In a letter printed in
the *Daily Mirror* on 26 July 1951, a woman wrote: 'After being
childless for many years, I was advised by a specialist to eat
plenty of lettuce, and to give my husband some too. In less than
six months my first baby was on its way.' Anyone for salad?

Lettuce might have helped Mary Page, who died in 1728; the
inscription on her gravestone reported that 'In 67 months she
was tap'd 66 times, had taken away 240 gallons of water, without ever repining at her case [complaining at her condition] or
ever fearing the operation.'

London's Foundling Hospital, financed by Captain Thomas Coram, took in and looked after unwanted children. On the day it opened, 2 June 1756, 117 babies were found abandoned outside its doors, and between that date and 1766 over fourteen thousand children had been cared for by the institution.

Whether the tumour found on the brain of Charles Whitman during his post-mortem was the cause of his appalling crime is open to doubt, but tumour or not, the fact remains that one day in July 1966, after shooting his mother and stabbing his wife to death, he climbed the 300ft high observation tower of the University of Texas at Austin, taking with him some sandwiches, peanuts and a radio, and proceeded to open fire with a high-powered rifle. Being a trained sniper, he had no difficulty in wounding or killing 46 people on the campus below. The area was evacuated and the police moved in, initially to no avail; even an attack by an aircraft proved abortive, and it was not until the police managed to force their way through the barricades he had erected that Whitman was killed in a hail of bullets.

FOR THE RECORD

The only American sentenced to be hanged, drawn and quartered for High Treason was Edward Gove in 1683. Taken to England, he was imprisoned in the Tower of London but was later reprieved by James II.

Between 1826 and 1840, 625 of those convicts transported to New South Wales and Tasmania were hanged, and nearly four million strokes of the lash were applied to the bare backs of those who broke the harsh rules in force.

Italy did not legally abolish torture until 1786.

The last public execution in France took place on 17 June 1939, when Eugen Weidmann was guillotined in Versailles for murder. So large and uncontrollable were the crowds at the scene that within a week the authorities issued a decree confining all future executions to the privacy of the prison yard.

A total of 12,460 women convicts had been deported to the penal colony of New South Wales by 1840, when such transportation was ended.

During the American War of Independence more than 1600 prisoners were captured by British forces and confined in prisons at Forton in Hampshire, Plymouth in Devon and Pembroke in South Wales. Captured VIPs were held in the Tower of London.

A number of American servicemen deserted during World War II, but only one, Eddie Slovak, was shot by firing squad, as an example to others.

Capital punishment was abolished in Queensland, Australia, in 1922, though continued in other states for many years.

The first multiple hanging to take place in the penal colony of Tasmania occurred on 28 April 1821, when ten men were executed for robbery.

Historian John Stow recorded that during the reign of Henry VIII, which lasted 38 years, 72,000 people were executed for one crime or another.

The first bank robbery to take place in the USA occurred in Liberty, Missouri, in February 1866.

The last public hanging in the USA took place in Kentucky in 1936.

Following India's Independence in 1947, the first woman to be hanged there was Rattan Bai Jain, for murder.

The greatest number of people hanged at the same time in England was 24 – 23 men and a woman – at Tyburn in 1649.

The last man sentenced to be burned at the stake in the USA was a slave named 'Negro Jack', the execution taking place in 1825.

Some ancient laws remain on the books well past their sell-by date. As recently as the 1930s in Maryland, USA, setting fire to a haystack was still punishable by death.

The largest number of victims hanged at the same time in the Western world was 38 Native Americans who were executed at Mankato, Minnesota, in 1862, after having massacred scores of settlers.

The last woman to be hanged as a witch in England was Alice Mollard, in 1686.

In France punishment by the pillory was abolished by law in 1832.

The statute requiring miscreants to be stripped naked when being whipped through the streets was mercifully modified by Elizabeth I, who decreed that they need only be stripped to the waist.

Bodies of dead women were used to test the effectiveness of the prototype guillotine.

There was once a hangwoman, Lady Betty, who enthusiastically performed that duty in Roscommon, Ireland, in the nineteenth century.

In Scotland in 1563 adultery was made a capital crime and those committing it were hanged in public.

Between 1930 and 1972 more than 3800 men and women died in the electric chair in the USA.

The first execution by electric chair took place in the USA in 1890, the victim being murderer William Kemmler.

The last witch to be executed in Germany was burned at the stake in 1775.

Reportedly the first execution by the axe in England occurred in 1076, when the Earl of Huntingdon was beheaded.

The last instance of burning at the stake in Germany took place in Berlin on 18 August 1786. The criminal, stripped to his shirt, was made to enter a cage-like frame, the door of which was then fastened; wood and straw were then heaped around the structure and ignited.

The first witchcraft trial to take place in England was in 1208, the prisoner at the bar being Gideon, a sorcerer; he was acquitted.

The last queen to be beheaded in England was Mary, Queen of Scots, in 1587.

The first person to be hanged, drawn and quartered in England was a pirate, William Marise, who was executed in that manner in 1241.

In England the medical dissection of the corpses of hanged criminals was not abolished until 1832.

The largest number of witches incinerated in one day in Germany occurred in 1589, 133 of them dying at the stake.

The last man to be publicly hanged in Scotland was Dr Edward William Pritchard in 1865.

The first person in Irish history to be burned at the stake for being a witch was Petronilla de Midia in November 1324.

The only triple hanging in Australia took place on 15 October 1883, when three men were simultaneously executed for murder.

The burning of heretics in England was legalised in 1401.

Although the last woman burned as a witch in Scotland perished in 1708, it was not until 1789 that England's witch-burning days finally came to an end.

Until 1834 any convict returning to England after having been sentenced to transportation for life to the colonies was hanged; after that date they were simply imprisoned for life.

The longest trial in English criminal history took place at Bedford Assizes in 1962 when James Hanratty was found guilty of murdering Michael Gregston on Deadman's Hill in Bedfordshire, and later hanged; it lasted 21 days.

The first banknote was issued by the Bank of England in 1694 but it was not until 1758, 64 years later, that forged notes appeared, twenty of them being manufactured by a Stafford draper in an attempt to impress a lady friend with his wealth. He paid the due price of the law.

John Archer was the last man to be racked in England, in 1640.

The first man to be guillotined in France was Nicolas-Jacques Pelletier, for thieving, on 25 April 1792.

It was not until the 1820s that the whipping of women became illegal in the United Kingdom.

The last two men to be hanged in Great Britain were Peter Anthony Allen and Gwynne Owen Evans, at 8 a.m. on 13 August 1964.

The only woman recorded as being tortured on the rack was Anne Askew, a Protestant, during the reign of Henry VIII.

The list of fatalities for the week 15–22 August 1665 in London totalled 5,568; among them were 18 who died from 'Rising of the Lights' [a stomach ailment], 79 from 'Griping in the Guts', 2 from being 'Frighted', 17 from 'Stopping of the Stomach', 4,237 from the plague – and one woman who 'Broke her skull by a fall in the street at St Mary Woolchurch'.

The last time the death sentence included hanging and beheading in the United Kingdom was in 1820, the victims being the Cato Street Conspirators.

In earlier centuries suicides in England were buried in unsanctified ground at crossroads with a stake driven through their hearts; the last to be so treated was John Griffiths, in London in 1823.

At Salisbury Assizes in 1830, of the 130 prisoners who faced trial, Mr Justice Gazelee condemned 29 to death, five to transportation overseas, five to fourteen years' jail, eleven to seven years' and the rest to various lengths of hard labour.

Throughout history typhoid has flourished, especially in wartime. During the Civil War in America there were no fewer than one thousand victims of the disease in every hundred thousand deaths.

The public whipping of women in England ceased in 1791, all public whipping being abolished in 1817.

The last woman to suffer in the ducking stool in England was Jenny Pipes in 1809.

Gunpowder was used for the first time in Western countries in 1330.

The first and only woman executed in Queensland, Australia, was Ellen Thompson for murder. When she was hanged, in 1886, the drop was too long, tearing her neck open and causing profuse bleeding.

The last woman in England to be condemned to death as a witch was Jane Wenham, who was later granted a royal pardon.

The last man to be publicly hanged in England was Michael Barrett on 26 May 1868 outside Newgate Prison, London.

The pillory was used in London until 1830, when the one situated outside the Old Bailey was removed.

Between 1749 and 1771, 678 criminals were sentenced to death at the Old Bailey and duly executed; of that number, 72 were hanged for murder, 251 for highway robbery and the remainder for burglary, horse-stealing, coining, shop-lifting, rioting and minor offences.

The last man to suffer in the stocks in England was Mark Tuck for being drunk and disorderly, in 1872.

The English law abolishing the hanging of criminals under the age of sixteen was not passed until 1906.

So far as is known, the only Western country to have the 'dishonour' of hanging a woman's cadaver in a 'sute of iron' on a gibbet is Canada; there, in 1763, that of a Mme Dodier was displayed as a deterrent after she was hanged in St Valier, Quebec.

In the years 1826 and 1827 no fewer than 103 hangings took place in Tasmania.

Torture was reportedly introduced in Denmark in 1157.

Being burned at the stake was rarely the fate of American colonists, and the only white woman to be so executed was Catherine Bevan, found guilty of murdering her husband.

Until 1875 chimneys were swept by 'climbing boys', some little more than children, who first clawed their way up the chimney, using their knees and elbows, then scraped away the soot, at times forcibly urged on from below by their masters. A Royal Commission in 1864 reported that 'No-one knows the cruelty a boy has to undergo in learning. The elbows and knees were deliberately hardened by rubbing them with the strongest brine, close by a hot fire. At first the boys would come back from work streaming with blood and the knees looking as if the caps had been pulled off – then they had to be rubbed with brine again!'

The only person in American judicial history to suffer *peine forte et dure* – being pressed beneath heavy weights or stones – for refusing to plead guilty or not guilty was eighty-year-old Giles Corey, accused of witchcraft. He still refused to plead, so was pressed to death in 1692. A contemporary recorded that as more weights were added, his tongue protruded from his mouth, whereupon the sheriff pushed it back in again with his cane.

Decapitation as a legal method of execution was introduced into England in 1076 by William the Conqueror, the first victim being Earl Waltheof.

The first woman hanged in the American Colony was Dorothy Talby in 1637, for killing her three-year-old daughter.

The first known martyr for the Christian faith was St Alban, beheaded by the Romans in about the year 293.

The first person to be hanged in Tasmania was Private Thomas England in 1806 for abetting in a robbery.

Owing to an oversight by the Scottish judiciary, it was legal until as recently as 1948 to sentence a condemned man to be hanged, drawn and quartered.

The last person to be publicly hanged in Canada was murderer Patrick James Whelan on 11 February 1869.

The last public executions to take place in the Tasmanian penal colony occurred on 27 June 1855, when four men were hanged for various crimes, none of them murder.

In 1349 the Black Plague decimated London's population of about 70,000, more than 25,000 inhabitants dying of the disease, many of their suppurating corpses lying in the streets awaiting burial in the plague pits.

In Scotland the first occasion on which a hanged man was subsequently hanged in chains, i.e., from a gibbet, was in March 1637, the felon being one MacGregor, sentenced for theft, robbery and murder.

The last execution by drowning in Iceland occurred in 1777.

The first murder to take place on a train in England was committed by Franz Muller, in 1864. He was hanged.

The only woman in the American colonies whose cadaver was suspended from a gibbet as a visible deterrent was Esther Rodgers, hanged in 1701 for infanticide.

It was not until 15 July 1820 that a law was passed abolishing the judicial flogging of women, in public or private.

Judicial execution by beheading was abolished in England in 1814.

The last man to be executed by the axe in England was Simon, Lord Lovat, in 1747.

The Statute of the Streets of 1595 ordained that 'No man shall blow any horn in the night within this city of London, or whistle after the hour of nine of the clock in the night, under pain of imprisonment. No man, after that hour, shall keep any rule whereby such sudden outcry be made, as making affray, or beating his wife or servant, or singing, or reviling in his house, to the disturbance of his neighbours, under the pain of being fined iiis. iiiid. [3s. 4d., or about 16½p].'

It is believed that the Paris catacombs contain at least three million corpses.

The English spent most of the eighteenth century fighting: in 1701 against the French; in 1715 and 1745 against the rebellious Jacobites; in 1718 they were at loggerheads with Spain; in 1741 the army was heavily engaged in Flanders; in 1753 they fought the French and Indians in America, and in 1777 against our colonists on that continent; in 1793 battles took place in the Netherlands; and in 1799 the army was more than busy in India.

The last woman to be executed in Tasmania was Margaret Coghlan in 1862, found guilty of murdering her husband; after seizing the iron bar with which he was attempting to strike her, she beat him with it, then cut his throat.

In the great San Francisco earthquake and fire of 1906, more than one thousand residents lost their lives, but only five hundred charred bodies were recovered from the shattered ruins of the city.

Before the electric chair was used to execute a human being, experiments were carried out on monkeys. They were successful.

The last person to be hanged for forgery in England was Thomas Maynard, in 1829.

Californian kidnapper Caryl Chessman holds the record for the longest wait before being executed: twelve years on Death Row in San Quentin.

During the French Revolution, between May 1792 and June 1793, no fewer than 1255 people were guillotined in Paris.

Hanging, as a judicial punishment, was first introduced into England by Edward III in 1334.

Until German law was changed in 1513, some criminals and the majority of adulterous women were executed by being buried alive.

The first American to be executed in the gas chamber was murderer Gee Jon in February 1924.

The last man in England to be gibbeted was James Cook in 1832.

In the 1920s the state of Idaho had a law forbidding the sale of chickens between sundown and sunrise, without first informing the sheriff.

Fifty-four persons were tried at the Old Bailey on 24 February 1732. Ten were sentenced to death, one of them being William West, aged 16, for burglary. All were hanged in public outside Newgate.

The last woman to be publicly executed in Dumfries, Scotland, was Mary Timney, hanged for murder on 29 April 1862, the executioner being William Calcraft, the official hangman from 1829 to 1874.

During the fourteenth century at least 25 million people in Europe died from the plague. In the Avignon region casualties were so great that graveyards could not accommodate the corpses, whereupon Pope Clement consecrated the River Rhône so that they could be deposited in its depths.

In Anglo-Saxon times a man declared an outlaw was literally outside the law; so far as civil law was concerned, he was dead and had no civil rights whatsoever. Until the thirteenth century, he could be killed by anyone, anywhere, and friends who dared to shelter or assist him could be similarly treated.

At the approach to many towns in eighteenth-century Denmark, visitors would be greeted by the sight of a whipping post erected at the roadside; incorporated on top of the post was a figure of a man with a sword by his side and a whip in his hand. Gibbets, complete with pendant bodies of executed criminals, also warned travellers of penalties, should they fail to behave.

In the twelve months ending 22 December 1603 the plague, which had been blamed on 'the air being infected with a certain venomous vapour contrary to the nature of man', killed 30,578 people in England.

The only woman ever hanged in California was a Mexican named Juanita, for stabbing a drunk who had broken into her house.

In the eighteenth century thousands of convicts were transported to the penal colonies of Australia, there to suffer so much hardship and suffering that in nine months a tenth of those in New South Wales died of disease and lack of proper sustenance.

A thirteenth-century fire precaution decreed 'That all persons that dwell in London's Great Houses within the ward have a ladder or two, ready and prepared to succour their neighbours in case of fire, that all persons who occupy such houses have, in summer time, before their doors, a barrel full of water for quenching fires, and that the reputable men of the ward, with the Aldermen, must provide a strong crook of iron with a wooden handle, together with two chains and two strong ropes [to pull the burning thatch down], and that the bedel [beadle, town official], have a good horn, and loudly sounding.'

The first successful course in the art of dissection given in the United States was conducted by Dr Shippen in Philadelphia in 1762.

In England condemned men were beheaded by the axe as recently as the nineteenth century, albeit after they had already been hanged.

The Spanish Inquisition reportedly burned more than thirty thousand 'witches' between the years 1450 to 1600.

During the 'Final Solution' devised by the Germans during World War II, at least five thousand people a day died in the gas chambers in one concentration camp alone. The gas, Zyklon B, brought death by suffocation within thirty ghastly minutes, after which the bodies were hosed clean and dragged out on to a conveyor belt, which then transported them to the crematorium.

To protect England's seventeenth-century wool trade it was forbidden for shrouds or coffin linings to be made of the traditional linen; those who flouted the law were fined the enormous sum, for those days, of £5.

The first time in British judicial history that a man was convicted of murder on the sole evidence of teeth prints on the victim occurred in 1948, when Joan Gorringe was found dead in Tunbridge Wells. In addition to other injuries, the teeth marks on her right breast were so unusual that casts were taken, and checks with local dentists led the police to the killer, her husband. He was sentenced to be hanged, but this was later commuted to life imprisonment.

On 18 July 1694 large crowds gathered at Tyburn to watch eleven men and three women hanged, most of them for coin-clipping.

When Arthur Prince, reportedly the first ventriloquist to master the art of drinking water while speaking through his dummy, died in 1948, in accordance with his wish his dummy was buried with him.

It is believed that the first person of Jewish faith to be hanged in the American colonies was Martin Weinburger in 1884 for murder.

During the Great Plague of 1665 the corpses of 120,000 victims were buried in Bunhill Fields ('Bone Hill' Fields), London, at a rate of five thousand a week.

The first time the Identikit system was used in England was in 1961, when murderer Edwin Bush was identified by means of the device and hanged at Pentonville Prison, London.

The first man in England to drive a car at 100mph was Percy Lambert. He was killed while trying to exceed that speed at

Brooklands racetrack in 1913, when a puncture caused his car to crash and overturn.

Among the Statutes laid down by the London authorities in 1562 against 'Noysaunces' (Nuisances) was one which stated that 'No Man shall cast any Urine-Boles (bowls) or Ordure-Boles into the Streets by Day or Nights afore the Hour of Nine in the Night; and also he shall not cast it out, but bring it down, and lay it in the Canel, under Pain of three Shillings four Pence; and if he do cast it upon any Person's Head, the Person to have a lawful Recompence, if he have Hurt thereby.' It was therefore advisable to wear a wide-brimmed hat if venturing forth after the Hour of Nine!

During the infamous slave trade, 71,115 Africans were delivered to Jamaica during the years 1751–61; they were sold for an average price of £30 each.

France abolished capital punishment in 1981, the last execution by the guillotine having been carried out in 1977.

In the 1700s, children aged between seven and fourteen who committed crimes which carried the death penalty were only hanged if it was believed they had acted intentionally, but if they were over fourteen, there were no mitigating factors: they were classed as adults and hanged like everybody else.

On 20 August 1612 nine of the notorious Pendle Witches were hanged at the same time on Gallows Hill, Lancaster.

The punishment of being flogged was abolished in France in 1789, but it continued to be part of naval discipline until 1848.

The last head reportedly exhibited on London Bridge was that of goldsmith and banker William Staley, hanged, drawn and quartered for treason in 1678. Such was the penitence he showed at his trial that originally permission was given for his body parts to be decently buried instead, but so loud were the Masses sung at his funeral in St Paul's Church, Covent Garden, that complaints reached the King, who promptly gave orders that the grave be opened, Staley's quarters be displayed on the City's gates and the head set up on the bridge.

The first reported bodysnatching incident in Scotland was in February 1678, when four gypsies were hanged and their bodies thrown into a deep hole; the next morning one was discovered missing and it was concluded that local 'chirurgeons' had had it removed for dissection purposes.

To prevent people applying for grants from more than one parish council, an Act of Parliament dated 1697 decreed that everyone receiving council benefits had to wear a badge on their right sleeve with the parish's initials.

Of the 568 men and 191 women transported to Australia in the First Fleet, only 23 died in transit, but of the 1,095 convicts who sailed in the Second Fleet, almost a quarter, 267, perished during the six-month voyage.

Living conditions and disease epidemics were so appalling in the mid-1800s that a newborn child of the working classes had only one chance in two of attaining the age of five; for a child of the middle classes, the chances were four in five. The average age at death for London's working classes was 22, but for the middle class, 27.

In the Middle Ages, French husbands who allowed their wives to beat them were made to ride through the streets on donkeys, facing their steeds' tails, much to the ridicule of their neighbours.

After World War II 242 Belgians were shot by their compatriots for collaborating with the Germans during their occupation of the country.

Claims for compensation are far from new. Among the amounts paid out for accidents on London Bridge in the 1700s were: 5s. paid to R. Ward in April 1736 'to get Anne Tully into the Hospital, having fallen and broken her leg'; in June, 1s. 2d. for 'getting a poor woman off the Bridge'; and later an outlay of 3s. was required to pay two porters 'for carrying the Woman home that went to drown herself'.

More than two hundred offences were punishable by death at the beginning of the nineteenth century.

The last official hangman, Syd Dernley, a friend of the author, died in November 1994. He assisted the late hangman Albert Pierrepoint, taking part in more than 25 executions.

According to ancient records, more than 50,000 people were executed at London's Tyburn between 1196 and 1783, when the execution site was moved to Newgate Prison.

The largest annual total of executions in the USA occurred in 1935, when 199 criminals were put to death.

Between 1889, when execution by electrocution was legally established in New York state, and 1927, 431 men and six women were sentenced to death. Two of the women and 266 of the men were executed; of the others, two died natural deaths, three committed suicide, two drowned during an attempt to escape and eleven were diagnosed as insane, while the rest had their death sentences reduced to imprisonment.

The only queen to be tried as a witch was Joanna of Navarre, consort of Henry IV. In 1422 she was imprisoned in Pevensey Castle for four years.

Death in the electric chair isn't always instantaneous; at the execution of James Wells in 1922, no fewer than eleven repeated surges of high-voltage current were required to kill him.

The largest mass murder to have taken place in the United States prior to 1973 was the slaughter of at least 27 young boys, tortured, mutilated and killed by Dean Corll. He was shot and killed by an accomplice, Wayne Henley, who received six 99-year sentences of imprisonment for his part in the murders.

Drowning was an early method of execution in Scotland. In January 1624 Helen Faa, together with ten other gypsy women, was drowned in the nearby loch for various offences.

The first man to be executed for anti-abortion violence in the USA was an unfrocked Presbyterian minister, Paul Hill, aged 49, who shot and killed 69-year-old Dr John Britton and his driver/bodyguard James Barrett, a retired air-force colonel, in Pensacola, Florida, in July 1994, using a pump-action shotgun. Hill's last meal consisted of sirloin steak, broccoli, baked potato, salad, cheese and bacon bits, orange sherbet and iced tea. Completely unrepentant, Hill died by lethal injection in September 2003; his hooded executioner received the equivalent of £100.

The last executions on Tower Hill, London, took place in June 1780 as a result of anti-Catholic riots instigated by Lord George Gordon; ex-soldier William M'Donald, a cripple, who had lost an arm, Mary Roberts and Charlotte Gardener were hanged in public.

The inventor of the modern water closet was Sir John Harington, godson of Queen Elizabeth I. He described his brainchild in a book published in London in 1596, entitled *A New Discourse of a Stale Subject called the Metamorphosis of Ajax*, the word 'jakes' being the accepted slang name for the loo in those days.

The last man reportedly hanged at Tyburn was John Austin in 1783.

The first time a human body was publicly dissected was in Venice in 1308.

Until abolished by law on 28 April 1832, French criminals and convicts were branded with the fleur-de-lys or letters denoting their crime or prison.

Anyone who wished, for whatever purpose, to dig up a dead body, could do so without fear of prosecution, for a body did not belong to anyone – until a law was passed in 1788 making it a crime. Before that date bodysnatchers, who stole cadavers for gain, extracted the bodies but always threw the shrouds back in the graves to avoid being charged with theft.

One of the shortest court trials in English legal history is believed to be that of Joseph Clarke, who pleaded guilty to the charge of murdering Alice Fontaine in 1929; it took just four and a half minutes. He was later hanged.

The first woman to die in the electric chair was Martha Place, executed in Sing Sing prison on 20 March 1899.

On Christmas Day 1847, 22 London policemen were found to be drunk. They were all dismissed.

Two incongruous memorials stand next to each other on London's Tower Hill. One is a monument to the 24,000 sailors of the Merchant Navy and Fishing Fleet who were killed during World War II and have no grave but the sea; only yards away is the public execution site where those condemned to death were hanged or beheaded.

The English law permitting women to be burned to death for husband-murder was not countermanded until 1790.

Earle Leonard Nelson murdered no fewer than 22 landladies, sometimes one every three weeks, in the USA and Canada, and was hanged in Winnipeg in January 1928.

Attacking someone with a knife or other lethal weapon while being disguised carried the death sentence in Tennessee in the 1960s.

The only actress interred in Westminster Abbey was Ann Oldfield in 1730; her maid testified that 'she was buried, in a Holland shift [petticoat], with a tucker and double ruffles of the same lace, a pair of new kid gloves and a very fine Brussels lace hat, and her body wrapped in a winding sheet.'

The last triple execution at Newgate prison, occurred on 9 June 1896, when Henry Fowler, Albert Milsom and George Seaman were hanged for murder.

The last woman in England to be burned at the stake for counterfeiting money was Christine Murphy, on 18 March 1789.

Many condemned men in the USA submit appeals against their death sentences, some as many as three or four times, but surely Edgar Smith holds the record; following his trial for murdering

15-year-old Victoria Zielinski in 1957 his lawyers raised no fewer than fourteen appeals, resulting in thirteen stays of execution. Eventually, in 1971, he was released from custody, but was soon back on charges of kidnapping and attempted murder. Imprisoned again, he finally admitted Victoria's murder.

George III (1760–1820) was the last monarch to bear the title of King of America.

The largest number of people broiled at one time in England was in 1531, when 25 Dutch Anabaptists, 19 men and six women, and two others, were burned on 27 separate stakes in Smithfield.

Hanging became the legal method of execution in England in 1334, during the reign of Edward III.

The largest number of victims electrocuted in one day in Sing Sing prison was seven, on 12 August 1912.

The first execution in New York of a person guilty of murder by administering morphine occurred in 1891, when Carlyle Harris poisoned his wife in that manner.

When, in May 1948, four-year-old June Anne Devaney was taken from a hospital in Blackburn, Lancashire, and murdered, every man in the town was visited by police and more than 46,000 sets of fingerprints were taken. Comparison with those left by the murderer yielded results, those of Peter Griffiths proving a match. Found guilty at Lancaster Assizes, he was hanged on 19 November 1948.

Forty-seven executions were performed in 1962 in the USA; of that number, 29 died in the electric chair, 15 in the gas chamber, but only three by hanging. Many believe that the last method is slower and therefore more agonising than the others, but this has not proved to be the case every time.

The first time wireless was used in a murder hunt was in 1910 when the captain of the ship carrying wife-murderer Dr Crippen and his lover to Canada radio'd the news about his passengers to London; the authorities then sent police on a faster vessel, and the wanted man was arrested when his ship docked.

The first man on record who is said to have 'courted death by over-indulging in the new habit of smoking tobacco' was Dr Fletcher, Bishop of London, in the late fifteenth century.

The first execution performed in Sing Sing prison, New York, was that of the misnamed Harris A. Smiler, on 7 July 1891.

The first woman to be executed by lethal injection was serial killer Margie Velma Barfield on 2 November 1984 at Raleigh, North Carolina.

The last man to be burned alive in England was Edward Wightman in 1612.

5,143 teeth were extracted in the London Hospital during 1844 – without anaesthetic, of course!

The first recorded motor accident in Great Britain that resulted in the death of the driver happened on Grove Hill, Harrow, on 25 February 1899.

Identification of criminals was very difficult in the early twentieth century, and Alfred and Albert Stratton must have thought they had literally got away with murder after robbing and killing elderly Mr Farrow and his wife. They did not realise, however, that they would enter the judicial record books by being the first persons to be convicted of murder by fingerprint evidence, for a thumb print left on a cashbox in the Farrows' apartment was a perfect match with Alfred's. Members of the jury were convinced, and both were hanged in June 1905.

No fewer than 164 acres of London's 460 acres of buildings were destroyed by German bombing during World War II.

The last person to be hanged outside Newgate prison before it was demolished was murderer George Wolfe on 6 May 1902.

Mass murderer Arnfinn Nesset not only poisoned more than 25 people between 1977 and 1980, a record in Nordic criminal cases, but also created another record, in that 150 witnesses testified at his trial, making it the longest in Norwegian judicial history.

The first person to be executed by lethal injection in the United States was Charles Brooks on 7 December 1982, having been found guilty of murder.

It was announced in 1949 by the British Government that all executions in Germany since the end of the war, 87 in number, had been by the guillotine.

SELECT BIBLIOGRAPHY

Andrews, W. *Old Time Punishments*, Andrews, 1890

Anonymous. *The Record of Crimes, Judgments, Providences & Calamities*, London, 1825

Barington, S. *Errors and Executioners*, David & Layton, 1909

Bell, W.G. *London Rediscoveries*, Bodley Head, 1929

Berry, J. *My Experiences as an Executioner*, Percy Lund, n.d.

Besant, W. *Westminster*, Chatto & Windus, 1897

Camm, Dom Bede. *Forgotten Shrines*, McDonald, Evans, 1910

Carment, J. *Glimpses of the Olden Times*, Jackson, 1893

Christeson, R. *Treatise on Poisons*, A. & C. Black, 1836

Cook, C. *Prisons of the World*, Morgan & Scott, 1902

Davey, R. *Pageant of London*, Methuen, 1906

Earl, A.M. *Curious Punishments of Bygone Days*, Macmillan USA, 1920

Eton, H. *Famous Poison Trials*, Collins, 1932

Gordon, C. *The Old Bailey & Newgate*, Fisher Unwin, 1902

Griffiths, A. *Mysteries of Police & Crime*, 3 vols, Cassell, 1899

Haggard, H.W. *Devils, Drugs & Doctors*, Heinemann, 1929

Hartshorne, A. *Hanging in Chains*, Fisher Unwin, 1891

Holinshed, R. *Chronicles*, 1586

Howard, J. *State of the Prisons*, Dent, 1929

Jackson, W. *The New & Complete Newgate Calendar*, London, 1818

John O' London. *London Stories*, 1926

Lawes, L.E. *Twenty Thousand Years in Sing Sing*, Constable, 1932

Machyn, H. *Diary of a London Resident*, Camden Society, 1848

Marks, A. *Tyburn Tree*, Brown, Langham, 1908

Schmidt, F. *A Hangman's Diary*, Philip Allan, 1928

Sanson, H. *Memoirs of the Sansons*, Chatto & Windus, 1876

Smith, E.T.M. *Roll-call of Westminster Abbey*, Smith Elder, 1903

Stanley, Dean. *Memorials of Westminster Abbey*, Murray, 1869

Swain, J. *Pleasures of the Torture Chamber*, Douglas, 1931

Taylor, G.R.S. *Historical Guide to London*, Dent, 1911

Timbs, J. *Curiosities of London*, Warne, 1855

Verdène, G. *La Torture* (French edition), R. Dorn, Paris, 1906

Wallace, W.S. *Canadian Murders & Mysteries*, 1931

Saturday Magazine series, 1833

Old and New London series Walter Thornbury

Gentleman's Magazine series (18th-century)

Police Gazette series

The Penny Magazine series

Catalogue of Torture Instruments from the Royal Castle of Nuremberg, Ichenhauser, 1893

Calendar of State Papers, Domestic Series

Tower of London Records

AUTHOR'S DETAILS

Geoffrey Abbott joined the Royal Air Force as an aero-engine fitter prior to World War II. He saw active service in North and East Africa, Somalia and India, post-war in the Suez Canal Zone, the Hashemite Kingdom of Jordan, Cyprus, Malta, Iraq and the Gulf States, and later served with NATO in France, Germany and Holland. After 35 years' service with the RAF he retired in 1974 with the rank of Warrant Officer and then, on becoming a Yeoman Warder ('Beefeater'), lived in the Tower of London and was sworn in at St James' Palace as a Member of the Sovereign's Bodyguard of the Yeomen of the Guard Extraordinary, and by Justices of the Peace as a Special Constable of the Metropolitan Police.

As an author of books on torture and execution, his qualifications are unquestionable, he once spent some time in the condemned cell of the high-security Barlinnie Prison, Glasgow, and later stood on the 'drop' trapdoors in that jail's execution chamber (as a fact-finding author, not a convicted criminal!). He also had the experience of having a noose placed round his neck by a hangman – the late Syd Dernley, a man endowed with a great, if macabre sense of humour!

Geoff now lives in the Lake District, where he acts as consultant to international TV and film companies. He has appeared in several documentaries on UK and American television channels. By invitation, he has also written the entries on torture and execution for the latest edition of the *Encyclopaedia Britannica*. In addition to being Sword Bearer to the Mayor of Kendal, Cumbria, he is learning to become a helicopter pilot.

OTHER BOOKS BY THE AUTHOR

Ghosts of the Tower of London
Great Escapes from the Tower of London
Beefeaters of the Tower of London
Tortures of the Tower of London
The Tower of London As It Was
Lords of the Scaffold
Rack, Rope and Red-Hot Pincers
The Book of Execution
(also Japanese version)
Family of Death
Mysteries of the Tower of London
The Who's Who of British Beheadings
Crowning Disasters
Regalia, Robbers and Royal Corpses
The Executioner Always Chops Twice!
Grave Disturbances
William Calcraft, Executioner Extraordinaire!
A Beefeater's Grisly Guide to the Tower of London
Lipstick on the Noose